Be the Director I Could Follow

Heres your
first award! ☺

Be the Director I Could Follow

A Camp Director's Manual

Earl D. Taylor

Co-authored
by

Enoch Olson, Brian Ogne, Tom Robertson
and Dick Angelo

Foreword
by
John Pearson

Cover design by:
Elly Mullen and Emily Fay

Be the Director I Could Follow

Copyright © 2016 Earl Taylor
All rights reserved.

ISBN: 6198626

ISBN-13: 978-1530981113

Dedicated to my wife, DeDe,
who has been
my constant helper
throughout our
thirty-seven years in camping.

Foreword

Harvard Business Review's classic article, "7 Surprises for the New CEO," is a wake-up call for both corporate and nonprofit leaders– including camp directors. Surprise Number Five is a shocker: "You Are Not the Boss." Few articles and books equal the honesty and warnings from these co-authors.

So I was blessed and privileged when Earl invited me to write this foreword. His written labor of love– transparently delivered with warts and all– is a valuable survival kit for new and growing camping leaders who will find not seven, but *dozens* of surprises in their leadership journeys.

Oh, my. How I wish Earl's wit and wisdom had been in print decades ago when I invested 11 immensely challenging (but thoroughly satisfying) years as a camp director in Illinois and Washington. *I would have read this book every week!*

Then when I was privileged to lead what is now called Christian Camp and Conference Association (CCCA), I would have gifted his book to hundreds of struggling (but amazingly committed) men and women who loved Jesus and led remarkable camping ministries.

Be the Director I Could Follow is a feast for new leaders and old leaders. In addition to Earl's savvy smarts from his in-the-trenches school of hits and misses, he's invited four of my Christian camping heroes (Dick Angelo, Brian Ogne, Enoch Olson, and Tom Robertson) to serve up their common sense approach to leadership. *Brilliant!*

Here are six reasons you MUST read this book– and share it with your team:

1. **Twitter-Worthy Quotations Sprinkled Throughout the Book.** *Amazing stuff!* Like John Maxwell's insight: "The only thing a title can buy is a little time– either to increase your level of influence with others or to undermine it."

2. **Brian Ogne's Four Principles of Funding Your Ministry.** My favorite: "People give money to success, not to distress."

3. **Tom Robertson's Transparent Confession.** "...I needed to settle the glory issue. Either I got it or God got it. I was not meant to carry the glory belonging to God. It was so freeing to lay that burden down."

4. **Enoch Olson's Sacred Task.** "As the visionary I had the sacred task of proclaiming a vision of a future that did not yet exist ... for a people with the means to bring that future into a present reality." (Note: Enoch wrote his chapter at age 85 and noted, "With the help of many, my style of leadership is still improving which means it is a growing process. There are real reasons why some leaders succeed and others fail.")

5. **Dick Angelo's 7-Day Prayer List.** "The best practice that a young or old director can get into is to take all the cares of the week, make a list of them, and daily spend time in prayer over them. Keep that list at least a week ahead all the time. That way, one prays for the need

today, as well as always praying for the needs of the next several days." *Yikes! How did I miss this discernment insight? While grace abounds, I wish I had started this 50 years ago, not this week.*

6. **Earl Taylor's Metric That Matters Most— the Happiness File.** "I do keep a close watch on the finances of the camp; without enough money, the camp begins to flounder and morale and facilities go downhill. Staff likes to be paid. But I have an even more important system to measure the success of the camp: it is called my 'happiness file.' In my desk, I keep a file of all the good reports I hear from parents, churches, and campers." *Great insight– great idea!*

Recently, I heard a millennial youth leader share this at a large conference. "Next month I turn 30– and it will be the fifth anniversary of that moment in my life when I discovered I didn't know everything!"

None of us know everything– but that realization is critical. I just learned a lot more and had several important nudges-in-my-ribs from the Holy Spirit as a result of reading *Be the Director I Could Follow.*

—*John Pearson*

Board Governance & Management Consultant

John Pearson Associates, Inc.
San Clemente, California
www.ManagementBuckets.com

Author's Note: John Pearson served from 1979 to 1990 as the executive director of Christian Camping International/USA (now CCCA). John is the author of *Mastering the Managing Buckets: 20 Critical Competencies for Leading Your Business or Nonprofit.*

TABLE OF CONTENTS

Born to Lead

I have always been a leader. Perhaps the mantle was thrown on me when my mother walked out of our family when I was five. I quickly learned that I needed to fend for myself if I wanted to get something done; I had no mom to wait on me as a small child. By age 12, my all-time favorite school teacher wrote on my end-of-the-year report card, "Earl can sometimes be bossy." My lot was cast early on.

One of my first jobs in high school was selling Fuller Brush; going door to door with a briefcase. Occasionally I was ostracized by a smart-aleck kid from my class. I made good money and became a top seller; most other kids were playing in band or going out for sports; I was learning to lead. I carried my Bible to school, proudly putting it on top of my stack of school books. I was alone in this effort. I started working 40+ hours a week while a junior in high school as a front desk clerk at the local Hotel Muscatine. I interacted with the town's big shots as they brought in business clients and guests. I watched others who led.

I attended college, edited the school newspaper, graduated with highest honors in the English department and I attended and finished graduate school.

Finally I accepted my first real job as an adult; I became a caretaker for a Girl Scout camp. I loved it at first. The job allowed me to start a family and to live on 360 acres of pristine hunting grounds. The job was not demanding: I mowed, I painted, and I greeted weekend guests and took care of their needs. I did what the Des Moines office told me to do. However, I did not get to lead; I had become a follower.

I left after five years. Perhaps I just knew that it was not a job that I wanted to do the rest of my life. Perhaps I knew I needed to use my gifts. At this time, there were no Meyers Briggs-type tests available to allow me to identify my talents and inclinations; I just knew in my heart that the job and the people I worked for had become unpleasant and unsatisfying to me.

I moved to another camp, a new camp that was needing some know-how. I had been sought out because I had five years of experience in a camp. Hidden Acres was needing someone to come alongside the executive director and help him develop this raw piece of ground. They were interested in my back and my brain.

I flourished. I started to lead. I started to spout off my opinion. I started to make decisions and change the direction of the camp. I started to have influence on how the camp was developed and operated. I was in my element.

But not quite; I was not in charge.

My strong personality and drive pushed me to lead. When I finally became the camp director, I knew I had found my calling.

How did I become the director that others would follow? Did I take leadership training? Did I major in leadership or management in college? Did I read a leadership book, attend a seminar, or buy a program to study? Nope... none of these. I was born this way.

I understand Psalms 139; I was fearfully and wonderfully made. Before a word was on my tongue, He knew me completely. I was who I am even before I was born... I was made this way!

Would I have become a leader if I had not accidentally fallen into camping? By all means. I was genetically coded to have the type of personality that is considered for leadership positions: I am resolute, bossy, opinionated, strong-willed, thick-skinned, unashamed, persistent, compassionate, and I had a big mouth.

Some of you who are reading this have been thrust into a position of leadership at your camp. Some of you grew into your position. Some of you were just willing to take the reins of leadership by default. We have all been placed into different roles: sometimes it fits, and sometimes it frustrates.

You have picked up this book after seeing the title, *Be the Director that I Could Follow*, in hopes that you can become a better leader. You were praying that by reading this, leadership skills would suddenly emerge after lying dormant for all these years. I hate to disappoint you, but if you have not been a leader up to this point in your life, you probably are not going to morph into one after reading one book. But it is a start.

I write this book to help you polish your already existing skills. I write this to give you a clearer picture of how to run your camp so that it can be self-sustaining and vibrant. I write this having experienced 37 years of being in two camps, growing and evolving and retraining myself to become a director that others would follow.

If you have been in your role as the camp director for a while, you have seen rather quickly if you had what it takes to lead. You have seen your staff being drawn to you for direction, or you have seen your staff go their separate ways doing things their way instead of yours. You have seen where you are weak, and you know where you stand out as a director. As John Maxwell so poignantly stated, "If you are leading and no one is following, you are simply on a walk."

We can be thankful that we are all made differently. God did know what He was doing when He created each of us. Trust me, not all camp directors are flamboyant and charismatic in their personality. Not all camp directors developed their skills as a leader the same way.

In this book, I have called upon four successful camp directors whom I personally know to share their story of how they led and directed their camp. From their stories you will see a pattern develop; you will see that underneath different personalities and styles, there are several common characteristics that these directors have developed or trained themselves as they grew into stronger and more effective leaders.

I was called. Some of you reading this were called as well; others of you were the last man standing and have been handed the mantle of the director. I purposely chose directors who have endured for at least 25 years to write their chapters; if they had not matured and grown their camps, their board would have released them. I know they were successful. They completed the task set before them. They finished the race. They never gave up.

Much of this book will provide insight on how to arrange systems and structure that create a growing camp. It will be your responsibility to settle into a particular style that fits your personality and your abilities. Each of these directors directed their way; they grew their systems and their culture to fit themselves. What worked for Enoch Olson will not fit you perfectly. What worked for Dick Angelo will only perfectly fit him. Take nuggets from all the writers and work it slowly into your own systems. Don't try to dump the entire book into your current camp operation.

This is written by a bunch of "old" guys who are "long in the tooth" and not up on all the new-fangled techno-driven fads of today. However, the heart of a child has not changed over the years – they are still in need of the outdoor, life-changing experience called the Christian camp. The insights of each director are even more applicable today and they are tested and proven to work. They will work for you as well.

Over my 37 years in camping, I personally have visited every camp that the four directors write about: what they say is what I saw and what I heard as I toured the grounds and got to know how they "ran camp!" During our infancy years at Hidden Acres I personally visited each of these camps or had the director come and consult and give me and our board direction and advice. I respect each one for their involvement in my own development and Hidden Acres' successes.

Just as my camp has benefited from outside eyes that have experience, I would like to help others. I am available to coach, consult, or just visit your camp and assist you and your board. I can be best reached at: *earldtaylor@yahoo.com.*

CHAPTER 1
Lead So Others Will Follow

"Victory awaits him who has everything in order–
luck people call it.
Defeat is certain for him who has neglected to take the
necessary precautions in time; this is called bad luck."

Roald Amundsen- *The South Pole*

No one wakes up in the morning and thinks, "I can't wait until I get to work so that someone else can tell me what I should do." Staff come to work each morning to be inspired, to be trained, to be a part of accomplishing a mission that is larger than themselves. This is why Christian camping is such a rich place to work for the layman: our work is Kingdom building. Being the director of a camp staff provides opportunity for leadership to develop.

Personally, I have tried all types of leadership styles. I have led from the rear, pushing and prodding staff to move in a particular direction. At other times, I have developed an idea into a program, and have been out front of the staff, putting the pieces together to make the program successful. I have yelled. I have chided. I have spoken softly and often. Every situation has brought out a different aspect of my leadership, but through it all, I remained the director. I remained the boss on top that made the final decisions. Not everything I did worked out correctly. Sometimes I had near-mutiny on my hands. Most often, my strong personality carried others into believing in my decisions.

God has placed you in your position as the director for a reason. If you were like me, once in the position, you knew you were in the right seat on the right bus. Others of you are still pondering if you have what it takes to keep everything going in one direction. You wonder if you might be a better follower than a leader. It is important to understand this. I consider leadership a gift. Scripture talks about some He gave to be pastors, or teachers, and others He gave the gifts of helps that come alongside others and make them successful. Know your gift.

I claim I was born that way. I claim I received a gene. That is only part of the equation. In grade school, I led the playground activities. I decided who played on whose team at recess. I made sure the slow and clumsy were included in games of touch football. Today, put me in a meeting where I am not running the committee, and I am as restless as a caged animal; I don't like NOT running the show. I don't make a good church board member.

However, you are not me. We are as different as night and day. You have a different skill set than I do. You could be quiet. You could be analytical. You could be pensive and reserved. You can still lead. You can still develop your camp and your staff into a great organization.

Peter Drucker writes this in his book, *The Effective Executive,* about five such habits of the mind that have to be acquired to be an effective executive:

1. *Effective executives know where their time goes. They work systematically at managing the little of their time that can be brought under their control.*

2. *Effective executives focus on outward contribution. They gear their efforts to results rather than to work. They start out with the question, "What results are expected of me?," rather than with the work to be done, let alone with its techniques and tools.*

3. *Effective executives build on strengths— their own strengths, the strengths of their superiors, colleagues, subordinates and on the strengths in the situation, that is, on what they can do. They do not build on weakness. They do not start out with the things they cannot do.*

4. *Effective executives concentrate on the few major areas where superior performance will produce outstanding results. They force themselves to set priorities and stay with their priority decisions. They know that they have no choice but to do first things first— and second things not at all. The alternative is to get nothing done.*

5. *Effective executives, finally, make effective decisions. They know that this is, above all, a matter of system — of the right steps in the right sequence. They know that an effective decision is always a judgment based on "dissenting opinions" rather than on "consensus on the facts." And they know that to make many decisions fast means to make the wrong decisions. What is needed are few, but fundamental, decisions. What is needed is the right strategy rather than razzle-dazzle tactics. These are the elements of executive effectiveness.*

What is Peter Drucker saying to the camp director? If you are going to be a director who is effective and one whom others will follow, you need to make great decisions that create results, building on the staff's strengths, while personally concentrating on a few major areas that you, the director, can perform with superior results.

Whatever your bent as a director, you must capitalize on your strengths, but in turn rely on the staff to complete you, and to create a camp staff that is unified around a common vision.

CHAPTER 2

Becoming the Director

If your gift is to encourage others, be encouraging. If it is giving, give generously. If God has given you leadership ability, take the responsibility seriously. And if you have a gift for showing kindness to others, do it gladly.

Romans 12:8 New Living Translation

So you want to be the director, do you? Are you sure you know what you are getting into? Do you understand what it takes to run a camp? Perhaps you were formerly the program director in charge of fun, and now you have been asked to replace the director. Now the work begins.

Here is a list of what you need to know. Air conditioning, backhoes, Bible studies, bulldozers, dishwashers, donors, electricity, finance, flower beds, food, hay, heating, horses, housekeeping, human resources, lagoons, marketing, office functions, plumbing, preaching, promotion, spreadsheets, tractors, tree planting, and writing newsletters.

Not only do you need to know something about all the things listed above, but now you have to get it all to work together as one unit moving forward. You have to know who does which job best. You have to know how much it costs to do this. And you will need to understand why you do or don't do that. It is complicated and there are many factors.

Now take a deep breath. It can be done. Others have managed all this at one time and provided the camp with the needed leadership and vision to grow and enlarge the camp's influence. So can you.

Where do you begin?

Drop to your knees and pray; pray hard and long.

Now get back up and read the rest of this book and keep praying every day that the Lord will give you clarity of thought, understanding of good systems, and a compassionate heart to lead. The Lord has put you where you are today and has a purpose for your leadership skills– settle in and rely on Him daily.

Very few of us have any training in professional camping. Some of us only attended camp as a child. We never worked for a camp as a counselor or even as a dish washer. We fell into the position by "divine accident." In my day as a 20 year old in college, there were few classes available on how to run a camp. (I was not aware you could be paid to work at a camp.) There were no classes on how to start a camp. We learned on the run.

So can you.

But this book is intended to save you some heartache, some headaches, and to relieve you of some painful backaches. It is intended to give you a bird's eye view from seasoned directors. No two directors ran their camps the same with the exact same mission statement. However, each director knew what he wanted to produce through their efforts: an opportunity for young people and adults to have their encounter with The Almighty while on their grounds called "camp."

In each of these different chapters written by four directors, you will find specific "hot button" issues that only they pursued. Some were more theological than others. Some grew the camp through their programs while others grew their camps with new buildings. Some directors were trained pastors while others were trained for something besides the ministry. Each brought a unique gift set to the job.

Each gift set was allowed to flourish. Each director charged ahead with whatever abilities and interests that he had ingrained in his young ambitious mind. Some of us jumped into the director's role without many gifts, but had the desire to be in charge and lead.

I say all this so that you can relax and be comfortable at your current position. You can be comfortable knowing that you don't need to know it all. You need to know the beginning, and you need to know the end; let's let a few experienced directors explain to you what it will take for you to last for 25+ years and to grow your camp into a sustainable, vibrant, growing organization that will continue to influence young people and families until the Lord returns.

Your current position may fall under one of these categories:

Position 1: You are either hired as the director, or you want to be hired as the director and you need some guidance. You need to know where to start and where to put your energy first.

Position 2: You are a director and you have land, buildings, equipment, program areas, and staff and you are wondering, how do you make it all fit together into a functioning organization that would be attractive to and effective for churches and youth groups?

Position 3: You have run into a wall and don't know whether to turn to the left or the right; you have taken the camp to its current level, but you cannot move past the here and now. You want to move it forward, but you simply don't know how.

Position 4: You are weary, tired, discouraged and broke. The camp is broke. The buildings are broke. You are on life support and want to breathe new life into your camp.

Keep reading, friend.

CHAPTER 3
I Will Follow You!

Perseverance and spirit have done wonders in all ages.
General George Washington

Becoming the leader that others could follow is pure hard work. Managing is easy. Managing is making daily decisions that tell the rest of the staff what should be done by the weekend. It tells the staff who to hire for the summer. It tells the builder to go ahead and buy the 100 squares of shingles to replace the chapel roof. Managing is taking care of today and tomorrow.

Leading is different. Leading means you must be consistent. Leading means you must be creative. Leading means you must be able to interpret the future with enough accuracy to warrant purchases or people.

Every one of us had days when we thought we were leading, but we were not. Every one of us has had days when all we wanted to do was follow someone else. We were too weary to care.

I like how various authors give historical examples of men who were leaders and explain how and why they are defined as a leader. Joel Miller, author of *The Revolutionary Paul Revere*, says Revere was a leader. Yep, the horse-riding, "British are coming" silversmith who was usually found hunched over a piece of silver was considered a leader when he: *"took the initiative, he leveraged his strength, he was reliable and he cultivated creativity."*

Nothing new with Miller's list of descriptions of Revere. Is Revere considered in the same breath as Washington or Jefferson? Hardly. But he did lead as he jumped on his horse and declared to those in Lexington and Concord, "The British are coming." He did create followers who prepared for the fight of their lives. Would the settlers have responded to Revere if he had been a wacky flake who was inconsistent in his work, or a big talker? I doubt it. His diligence and integrity as a businessman transferred him into being a leader, when called upon.

Sometimes leadership does develop under crisis. It did for Revere. Sometimes leadership is grown from a myriad of life experiences. All leaders are created differently, which means everyone **could** develop into someone others would follow.

Camp directors wear two hats: they are leaders and they are managers. The days you are managing, you don't feel like the leader, you feel like the boss. "Do this! Fix that! Make sure the sidewalks are shoveled, set up tables, tear down tables." Sounds more like a manager to me. A leader should be back in the office plotting out the next 10 years or something more important than worrying about the overflowing garbage cans in front of the main lodge.

You feel like you are on one of those playground apparatuses that swing back and forth. Leader- manager. Manager- leader. Roles change so quickly, you don't have time to switch hats.

Managing well actually creates the path to leadership. John Maxwell writes about this in his book, *The 5 Levels of Leadership*. You enter a job with a position – a title– and you are in charge over others. You are the camp director. You develop some skills, make some good decisions and choices and you move to the next level: the level where you are given permission to lead others. You are doing the job with such skill and you work so well with others that other people begin to give you permission to lead them. They come and ask you questions about the job. They look to you to create the schedule and work load, and they trust your judgment with other things. This is a fun spot in leadership for a young person.

Maxwell goes on and writes, "Your next level in leadership is production: where making things happen separates real leaders from wannabees." When a camp director hits this level of leadership, the camp is moving forward. All eight cylinders are clicking! There is movement. Action. New buildings. New staff. Better and bigger programs. This is the level that the world sees and takes notice and says, "She is quite the director! Great things are going on outside of town at that camp! She gets things done!" This is a great position to be in, and sometimes, it will be as high as a director will go. I stayed in this level for nearly 25 years.

Eventually you move into what Maxwell calls the Level 4 leader. This is the people development stage, where you invest in staff around you, building into them skills of leadership. It takes years to be able to get there for most directors. And finally, Level 5 is where you are developing leaders to be level 4 Leaders – very few make it to this level. I know that Dick Angelo and Enoch Olson are on this level.

Why bring up Maxwell's 5 Levels? It is important to understand where you are as the director. In reality, during the first few years, you are a Level 1 leader, but with growth and good judgement, you move into Level 2. When a director gets stuck at Level 2, he usually has plateaued and becomes ineffective. Sometimes camp boards will dismiss him with this statement: "We need to go a different direction." They are not saying the director is a bad person, incompetent, or a poor leader. They are saying he hasn't moved up and begun to produce – to make things happen around him.

One of my favorite words is production. Meaning– output. Results. New stuff. Create. Build. Expand. Directors who want to lead from Level 2 are status quo-ers or managers of other people's ideas. Not bad, but status quo existence quickly becomes sub-par through natural atrophy.

Know that there are different levels, and know when you were hired you were a Level 1 leader. Know that if you do enough things right, others will allow you to coach and direct them at Level 2. But please don't be content here. It is a great level to build skills and add depth and width to your understanding of camp, but if you can't make things happen that create energy, growth, and weekends filled with families and youth, you won't last for the long haul.

CHAPTER 4

Six Myths of Leading a Camp

The leaders thought in terms of reality, and they won in my book. They looked at what was, not what they wanted things to be. In your own leadership, face reality first. Get the bad news first. Really listen to the financial problems, personnel issues, and sales dilemmas. Good leaders think about reality first and then find solutions and opportunities second.

John Townsend - *Leadership beyond Reason: How Great Leaders Succeed by Harnessing the Power of Their Values, Feelings, and Intuition*

You've attended CCCA sectionals and maybe a couple national conferences and now you have been asked to become the director of a camp; it looked easy from the outside. "When I am in charge, it will be a piece of cake!" you declare. You believe in certain myths that led you to this naïve idea that camp director equals easy.

Myth 1: *When I am in charge and the director, I can just tell others to do all the work.*

Not a good plan, friend. You are setting yourself up to have your clay feet smashed quite quickly. Sure, camp directors can delegate jobs. Yep, we get to make the final decisions about purchases, hires or new buildings. The buck stops with the camp director.

Camp directors better come into the job with the mindset of "I can and will do all things that I expect the staff to do." First-time camp directors don't become CEO's of camps with 50 staff members at the beginning of their careers. They get a ma and pa camp. If they are lucky, maybe a camp with a maintenance man and an office lady along with a part-time cook and housekeeper. If this director is going to survive, he is going to get dirty, he is going to jump in the camp car and run off and do camp presentations to the Awana kids, and he will stay up late running off brochures or working on a weekend schedule. You are it, man, and it is sink or swim. You make it all happen.

Myth 2: *Directing a camp is pure fun, just like attending summer camp or coming to men's retreat in January.*

Oh boy, how wrong you are. Attending summer camp is great fun. Running summer camp is just that: running. And the running never stops until the last camper leaves. Sometimes, it goes from running to scrambling. Other days, the only thing keeping it together is the seat of your pants. It begins in earnest in January with the hiring of staff and writing of curriculum. It runs through the promotions months of winter and spring. It culminates with staff arriving and staff training. It finally ends sometime in August.

As far as men's retreat – when you are the director– you might not even get to hear the speaker or play one activity over the week-end. You are going to be swamped keeping track of it all. I hope you find time to sit down and eat one meal.

Myth 3: *If I have an idea it will happen.*

Ha! Have you told your board your idea? Have you introduced this great idea to the staff? Great ideas are easy to come by – they are a dime a dozen. Great ideas that get from your mind to reality will take some work, some planning, some compromising, and some sweat. Great ideas need approval, financing, staffing, and constant management to make "the idea" successful.

Myth 4: *If I build it they will come.*

It was true in Iowa with the baseball diamond. It may or may not be true at your camp. It does take new buildings with beds in order for people to want to come to your camp. And they want to eat and they want to meet and play in your buildings. In order to have great buildings that fit people's needs, the building need to be designed properly and located in the right place. After building a building, there needs to be a quality staff in place to provide great customer care. If you don't build, you can be assured no one will come and sleep on the ground at your camp, but just building a structure doesn't mean you will create and maintain a great business.

Myth 5: *Every donor will love to give money to my projects.*

Nope! I wish, but history doesn't prove that. Some donors will give. Some donors won't. Donors are great people with great hearts, but not all projects or needs touch them the same. Not all camp presentations will resonate equally with the 70-year-old couple who are in the process of allocating their future estate to non-profits. Donors look at past history to determine future results – if your camp has been successful in developing buildings in the past, donors understand your track record. If your camp has had some fizzles and flops in raising money for your ideas, their checkbook might remain closed.

Myth 6: *It should only take one or two years to turn this camp around.*

It only takes one or two years to get started turning a camp around and showing growth, but it takes years of steady management to keep it growing. Spurts and sputters are not turn-arounds. When you begin the process, you can assume you will never stop improving and building your camp – the work is never done.

Non-Myth: *And in conclusion to all the myths I have listed, here is one non-myth:*

It is worth every second of your efforts. All the work, all the time, all the energy you need to pour into making camp a life-changing experience for your guests is completely worth your time. All it will take is one 10-year-old boy to come up to you while you are racing around on your golf cart and tell you about his "encounter with The Almighty" the night before around the campfire. Your energy levels will skyrocket and you will be ready to continue for another year.

CHAPTER 5
My Story - Enoch Olson

Enoch Olson was the founding director of SpringHill Camps in Evart, Michigan. Enoch was 85 years old when he wrote his chapter. This one chapter could be a syllabus for a class in Christian camping. On a personal note: I consider Enoch to be one of the patriarchs of the modern day Christian camping movement. He gave advice to the Hidden Acres board prior to the purchase, and he was the keynote speaker at our dedication of the camp. www.springhillcamps.org

(Author's Note)

We were privileged to start SpringHill Camps with only a vision that excited people, eight interested leaders, 515 acres with 12 small lakes, beautiful woods, fields, and some buildings that made up Spring Hill Farms.

In 1969, our first year, we started with two small camps, 256 campers, a volunteer staff of about 30, mostly from a CE class at Trinity College, three churches, a great cook, many committed excited people and a great number of "miracles" from a Sovereign God.

The year I gave up my executive directorship was 1995, but I am still involved as a consultant. The staff we had to recruit had grown from the 30 to about 500 to 600. Now at 85 years old I am starting the development of a new day camp facility in Ludington, Michigan called Turning Point Adventure.

This year, SpringHill will see about 51,000 campers in both resident and day camp programs.

WHAT HELPED GROWTH

There is not just one thing that caused SpringHill to achieve its mission successfully, but many. I will list some of them, not in detail or in order of importance. I believe that they will be the foundation for you as it was for us. The Growth Engine that led to our success had six key elements. Each had its critical part in achieving our mission.

1. Our **Mission** would determine the results we would seek:
   - The mission would define our reason for existence. For example: my present mission is to reach every child in the Ludington area with the Gospel of Jesus. To accomplish our mission would demand a vision that would define all the activities that would produce results.

2. Our **Vision** would determine the direction we would travel:
   - "As the visionary I had the sacred task of proclaiming a vision of a future that did not yet exist ... for a people with the means to bring that future into a present reality." The vision was a picture of the future that created passion within the present people. It included the drawing power that made our ministry possible as it fulfilled our mission. Our vision statement provided direction, a shared goal, a target for us to achieve, and would give

us direction to where we were going as we charted the course. Our vision would then demand the people with the necessary resources to make it happen.

3. The **Personnel** we would gather would determine our potential:
    *   Because these people were so important, we continually draw people with the means to bring the future vision into reality. We knew that these people would make our ministry possible or impossible. The gathering of people became a constant priority, so we searched for those people with their gifts, abilities, skills, creativity, and their resources, to achieve the mission and vision. These gathered people would then demand a morale that would excite passion.

4. The **Morale** then would determine the relationships we would experience.
    *   This needed morale required spiritually mature people who were drawn together, united and excited for the cause, and empowered to achieve both mission and vision. This morale required the building of character with life skills and leadership development. It required that everyone understood God's big picture with educational excellence, creative teaching and a powerful curriculum. This kind of morale demanded a gifted and skilled leader who could teach and empower people to teach the deep truth of God and His plan in a creative way that transforms lives.

5. It would be our **Leadership** who would determine true success:
    *   Our leadership needed to have special skills as coordinators in drawing together receptive followers. They

needed to be great coaches who would build productive teams. They would need to be a catalyst that would create other trained, energized leaders. But if a leader is to do all this it would demand the right structure that could give the freedom to do what growth would require.

6. The **Structure** our leadership needed to build would determine process and the size we would become:

   - Many camps start with the wrong structure as did SpringHill. We began to realize that the system of by-laws and principles we were operating under would not allow us to grow. The structure was designed for control and not for growth. The right structure, which is the process of building, was not in place.

   - We needed a structure that gave power to lead, to influence followers, and not to limit that power. We needed a structure that would give authority to make decisions, to acquire resources, to gather personnel, to build morale, to develop teams, to energize leaders. Without that authority, leadership became frustrated in trying to assume responsibility they could do nothing about. They needed the freedom to create and not be limited as to what we could do or not do. So the structure was changed and SpringHill grew incredibly.

   - In reading Acts 2:17, I kept asking if I was to be the young man who created visions or the old man that only dreamed dreams. Dreams determine failure, because a dream is the death of a vision. A dream is a mission that could have become a reality but didn't. A vision is a mission that can become a reality. May you always create your vision and not be content to only dream dreams.

- Over the years we have helped many other camps re- structure for growth.

LEADERSHIP STYLE

I believe a leader must live out what they believe to be import- ant. With the help of many, my style of leadership is still improv- ing which means it is a growing process. There are real reasons why some leaders succeed and others fail. Here are some of the reasons for both success and failure.

- Most will acknowledge that the true measure of leader- ship is influence. You have to be able to sell vision and draw people and when you speak people will listen. I have found that people follow leaders who are stronger than themselves. I also found that who you are will be the kind of people you will attract. If I could not touch their heart I could not ask them for their help. People buy into who I am as a leader before they would get excited by my vision. People want to know where you are going before they will follow. If you are uncertain about the future people will not follow.

- The people who were in my inner circle were very im- portant, because my potential was determined by those closest to me. I learned to select them carefully. My re- sponsibility as a leader was to raise up other leaders by building up a trust that created followers.

- Someone once said, "Anyone can steer the ship, but it takes a leader to chart the course." Charting the course has been my joy, mainly when you arrive at the right destination. In all of that, I had to learn how to find a way for our teams to win by giving them power to be creative in achieving what they saw as their mission. It was difficult for me because I am a doer and have high standards. I had to be secure in letting go and giving power.

- In writing reports it is easy to list all of our achievements which may not be true results at all. If you have poor goals you will have poor reports. That is why we must seek results as a priority in achieving our mission. Results need to be celebrated and when your camp is on the move, momentum will be your best friend. But remember that in all good things we must strive to exceed expectations, for in so doing you create their excitement of the "wow."

- Growth is the balance between change and continuity. Camps are the element of change while the church is the element of continuity. Change is critical, for if you fear change, failure will be your outcome. Yet it is important for us to control the risk factor in change, because too much change creates chaos. I believe that change demands continual evaluation. Change should become "doing things better," but if something isn't working you can't keep trying to make it better. You can't make a failure better. Great change demands both creativity and imagination; if you have neither you cannot achieve.

- There are some things I have discovered to be important. Do not forsake the basics, because they are the foundation upon which you build. Do everything possible not to make false assumptions. Many leaders fail because they do not get all the facts before making key decisions; and know that ignorance is never an excuse.

- One of my strong leadership skills has been the ability to build alliances. We need connections with other organizations and people. If you don't, you will find yourself traveling alone.

- One of our major responsibilities is finances. If we cannot raise the needed resources or control the spending, failure is certain. Something I have learned that is very important is that people are not equal. Some have greater abilities to help than others, so we must be wise in our asking, know our people, become close as friends and celebrate with them the blessing of God-given results. One final suggestion, gratitude and the sharing of thankfulness – hand-written or a specially delivered thank you has no substitute.

BOARD RELATIONSHIP

I have found it important to work closely and regularly with the executive board so to clear all major change decisions with them before meeting with the general board. It was important to establish the needed trust and support so there were no surprises. Communicate often.

- If you have a voice in who is to be a board member, choose wisely. I have found that business leaders who make hard and fast decisions every day are more progressive in moving the camp forward because that's what they do in business. They do not struggle with the risk factor which is required for growth. Some professionals slow the process with too many detailed questions.

- You should choose leaders whose personal mission is the same as the mission of the camp.

- Always prepare fully. What you don't answer in your presentation will be asked. Sell results which answer the question, "why?"

ADVICE TO NEW DIRECTORS

Obtain and master the greatest theological training possible so you can teach and empower others. The greatest camping skills learned are not enough. Your teaching and training will make all the difference in the quality of your staff. Wherever I go, former staff members thank me continuously for the rich practical theology they received at camp. The training of the staff became one of our greatest ministries.

- Seek first to achieve ministry results over activity achievements and then celebrate and sell those results with the people.

- Create great drawing power by providing the most creative and exciting activities and housing. Always exceed expectation. Kids want exciting activities, but parents want better kids.

- Do something major and new each year that betters the camper experience. Ask parents to help you make the choice, then they will help you achieve it.

- Your primary mission should be to glorify God in achieving His plan and purpose for the world.

- Our ministry goals and objectives that became my priority have not changed in all our years. Our goals were:

    a) To send each camper home to face life with a new or renewed commitment to Jesus Christ.

b) To send each camper home to face life with resources and skills to stand by their commitment: how to study God's Word, how to pray, how to witness their faith, etc.

c) To send each camper home with a greater understanding of the meaning of life and how to achieve it.

d) To send each camper home with memories of joyful, wholesome, exciting, fun experiences in adventure and discovery apart from what the world says is necessary to have fun.

e) To send each camper home to face life with greater life skills in moral development.

f) To send each camper home to face life with a vision of Christ's Kingdom and their place in it.

- If you achieve your ministry goals and mission you will excite many people:

  a) We excite happy Parents by helping them raise better kids.

  b) We enhance Families by helping them produce better kids.

  c) We strengthen the Church by training and equipping better kids.

  d) We build God's Kingdom by multiplying better kids.

  e) We enrich the Community as they experience better kids.

  f) We empower the Next Generation by providing better leaders.

MY BEST CHARACTER ATTRIBUTES

I have chosen 19 character qualities I am continually working on. They are truly enablements from God's indwelling Holy Spirit. None come easy with a fallen sinful human nature.

In the "Stop Signs" of Life, I learned that in all circumstances I must trust the Sovereign God. God's sovereignty provides me with the proper perspective with which to view all of life. If we get the sovereignty of God straight, our lives and our ministries will rise to a new higher level.

- In our weakness God provides Strength
- In our discouragement God provides Comfort
- In our fears God provides Confidence
- In our questions God provides the Big Picture
- In our limitations God achieves the Impossibilities
- In our responses God provides a reason to Worship

BEST GIFTS, SKILLS AND ABILITIES

Gifts are God-given, skills are learned, and abilities are still being discovered. I am very relational, a creative visionary, a man of faith, positively optimistic. I have become a good teacher, and I can make things happen. I love to achieve what others say is impossible, but must be careful that achievement is not my goal.

- I have also discovered that those positive gifts become a liability if not controlled by the Spirit of God.

BIGGEST CHALLENGE TO OVERCOME

Being a creative visionary, management was not my strength. Just after starting SpringHill, a board member who was a leader at IBM gave me nine books on management and told me to read them all. I did and became forever thankful. Being in a management position required an aptitude for dealing with the many diverse aspects of interacting with people and I had to care about the people on a personal level as well as their ability to accomplish key responsibilities. I had to work on these nine traits I had to become a better manager:

1. Excellent Communicator
    - I learned that I must make communicating with my employees a priority. I had to share with them what I knew that they needed to know. I needed to be present on the job where they were and I needed to talk to them! A friend of mine was president of a large business in our small town and everyone loved him because he was out with them, continually listening and helping. This became my caring and learning process.

2. Good Team Builder
    - Building strong teams makes a productive work environment. Gaining team leadership skills made me able to take individual people and turn them into a collective unit that enjoyed achieving shared goals. It became my responsibility to train each team leader so they could lead.

3. Great Leader
    - I had to learn how to inspire and influence the behaviors of others by gaining the respect and confidence of those I worked with. I had to demonstrate the quality of character I desired in them. There are great books that will help you learn how. Read and outline them carefully.

4. Influential Mentor/Coach
   - Each of my staff were on a developmental journey and I had the responsibility of mentoring, coaching and encouraging them along their journey.

5. Effective Time Management
   - The hours in the day are never enough, and there are always unpredictable events and demands that derail the best intentions, so I had to develop efficiency in our work time and help my employees with their time management skills.

6. Master the Details
   - The big picture is vital. Being a visionary and a big picture person, I had to learn how to master the details that were necessary even though I hated to do so. I was a great starter and had to learn how to become a good finisher. Mark, my son, was a great finisher and taught me much.

7. Set Measurable Goals
   - Goals are how objectives are met and a mission is accomplished. I had to learn how to write ministry and organizational goals that supported our mission and help my employees do the same. Goals help me visualize in advance what the desired ministry results would look like when achieved or when not achieved. If an organization's ministry goals are too broad and all-encompassing or too nebulously defined, they will serve little purpose in charting a clear and united course of action.
   - Here are some helpful insights I found in developing ministry goals:

a) Ministry goals are value statements that reflect the issues the ministry organization holds to be critically important.

  – Goals must reflect mission, purpose and core values.

  – Goals must reflect the Biblical imperatives accepted as divinely directed.

  – Goals must reflect the key theological convictions held as absolutes.

  – Goals must reflect the basic major convictions of our faith.

  – Goals must consider the cultural influences that challenge success.

b) Ministry goals are achievement standards that define and measure success.

  – Goals must be a vivid description of desired results, a base for measuring success.

  – Goals must express the conditions they would like to become a reality.

  – Goals should be life relevant, defining results in visual behavior terms that are measurable.

  – Goals must be specific enough to minimize the need for continual subjective interpretation.

c) Ministry goals are management tools that guide the ministry organization in all its development and operations.

  – Goals must be the base upon which all present and future activities and development are built. Nothing is done without a reason.

- Goals must unite all administrative action with policy direction.
- Goals must establish the reason and priorities for all the organization's objective accomplishments.

8. Provide Feedback
   - I learned that frustration with performance that did not meet my expectations was my problem, and that I needed to communicate more clearly what was expected. It was my responsibility to provide the consistent feedback necessary in good management.

9. Fair and Unbiased
   - We all come to the workplace from different backgrounds and with unconscious biases due to our individual experiences. I had to learn to identify those personal biases and not allow them to influence how my employees were managed. Being objective when dealing with employees was imperative in fair management practices.
   - It is important to manage people and not solely their time at work because it is the people who produce results.

Here are a couple more thoughts on overcoming big challenges. Being a severe dyslexic with a phonetics hearing disability, so that I could not hear certain sounds, I was unable to spell. Even though school was hard I was able to receive degrees in education and theology. I had to find and trust people who would help me do what I could not do. I know that with God all things are possible. Today, I am still encouraging those with disabilities, assuring them they can achieve their goals. Many have learned how to live life with a God perspective that allows them to achieve the impossible for God's glory.

The death of my wife the second year as founding director of SpringHill, and the death of my son who took over as Executive Director in my place created challenges that demand a trust in a Sovereign God. Problems you can solve, but facts of life you must accept with grace.

ADVICE TO NEW DIRECTORS

The great desire of my heart was to become a man of God: The prayer of Jesus in John 17 has become my heart's desire, because what Jesus prayed were His desires. It reveals to us what a man of God desires for his life.

I encourage others to get to know the men of God who have led God's people to achieve God's mission, and how they became that empowered person of distinctiveness. Most have failed miserably along the journey, but through God's grace they gained a God perspective about life, a God-given purpose that changed everything. And so becoming "men of God," they were used of God to achieve the purpose God had chosen them to achieve. From history we discover that these men of God were ordinary people who hungered to know God and experience His presence. They had a transforming understanding of Who God is. "Who among the gods is like you, O Lord? Who is like you, majestic in holiness, awesome in glory, working wonders?" Exodus 15:11

Teaching is critical. I would get the best theological training possible so you can teach, train, equip and empower others. You can know all the camping skills available, but if you can't empower others with The Truth, you will only achieve things and not produce mission results. Because it is the second time I have said all this, please realize just how important I find it to be.

Take time to read much and think much. You need to design "think time" into your schedule or you will never end up doing so.

I tried to select the eight most important things I learned in moving SpringHill off the ground. I give you only an outline even when so much more could be said about each.

1. You must put priority on results: Ministry results are the most critical thing we do in Christian camping. It is the basis of measuring success. It is the core of all programming activities. It is the excitement of marketing. It is the cause appeal for development. It is the unifying passion of all staff personnel. It drives the operation and makes everything we do easier.

2. Dream big dreams until they become a vision from God.

3. Major on the basics, because they become foundation for everything else you do.

4. Work to peak your performance because quality will always bring rewards.

5. Prioritize leadership because they are the people who set the standard.

6. Stimulate the drawing power because that is the only way you will have those to minister to.

7. Overcome the fear factor because fear is closely tied to a lack of faith and trust.

8. Gratefully express thankfulness always because it is designed to replace many of our problems.

SUCCESSFUL METHODOLOGY

Your Philosophy of Camping must be thought out carefully. The following was mine at SpringHill:

1. *SpringHill draws a child from the routine of daily living...*
   - Without drawing power there is no one to minister to. So we will do whatever it takes to draw a child from the routine of daily living by creative housing, exciting activities in adventure and discovery, standards of excellence that exceeds expectations, powerful results that excite parents, and

2. *Places that child into a new purposeful change environment...*
   - SpringHill creates an environment where change is not just possible but real.
   - Growth is the balance between change and continuity. SpringHill is the change element that creates change in schedules, voices, experiences, etc.

3. *Controlled by new quality voices called staff...*
   - The spiritual training of staff became one of my main priorities

4. *Who creatively teach and model the message of Jesus Christ...*
   - Great rewards came from in-depth Bible teaching – deep truth taught simply.
   - We developed powerful teaching materials. As we themed each day we gave kids God's big picture which produced great results. This we have not changed in all our years.

- Monday– Discovering the Meaning of Life– God and Creation
- Tuesday– Understanding the Mess of Life – The World we live in of sin and depravity
- Wednesday– Trusting the Rescuer of Life – Jesus and Good News
- Thursday– Experiencing the Enabler of Life– The Indwelling Holy Spirit
- Friday– Taking in the Breath of Life – Sent home to spend 30 days in God's Word

5. *Through small relational, enjoyable learning experiences...*
    • We created a powerful philosophy of education that involved teachable moments in the process of knowing, doing and being.

    • By working with Michigan State University we were able to learn and design a creative teaching process based on how children learn.

    • SpringHill won great awards in Michigan for its educational philosophy.

6. *So that each child returns home transformed by God's Spirit...*
    • The many powerful results that made "better kids."

7. *To live out God's purposes through a personal relationship with Jesus Christ.*
    • In this we celebrated often at camp and received great praises from homes and churches.

VOLUNTEER ENGAGEMENT STRATEGY "A WORK OF HEART"...NINE TIPS FOR ENGAGING YOUR VOLUNTEERS

We all know volunteers have great value if there is an engagement strategy. In some ways all of God's Kingdom people are volunteers because they have chosen to serve The Most High Triune God. Volunteers then provide free labor for camps, and the secret to recruiting and retaining great volunteers is to keep them engaged with a feeling of ownership. This requires a volunteer engagement strategy which is based on the camp's ability to help them feel like what they do adds value, helps fulfill the mission and that they make a difference.

Camps that do a good job of engaging their volunteers find that the volunteers are excited about what they do and give more than is asked of them. Engaged volunteers are committed to a vision, the cause and serve as advocates for the camp. However, when volunteers are not engaged they lose interest quickly and will eventually step down from their role.

1. *We provided volunteers an exciting mission and vision-* Engaged volunteers are committed to a vision. Volunteers do what they do because they rally behind a cause they believe in with passion.
2. *We provided volunteers structured communication-* Structured and consistent camp communication is one of the most important things a camp can do to foster engaged volunteers. Volunteers who give of their time and a portion of their lives have a natural interest in what is happening behind the scenes. They need to see the big picture as they serve.
3. *We provided volunteers interaction with a supervisor-* Never underestimate the value of supervisor interaction.

These interactions also create a great opportunity to learn ways the camp can better support the volunteers. Volunteers want to know that they are cared for as individuals – so asking about their families, their jobs, their hobbies or other personal interests makes them feel valued. We found it necessary to have a full-time supervisor just for our volunteers.

4. *We provided volunteers development opportunities-* Engaged volunteers value opportunities to develop and grow in their roles. Camps that utilize large numbers of volunteers need to be constantly looking for ways to develop and promote them to leadership positions. A great danger is that staff can become self-sufficient or micro-manage the teams and lose valuable human resources God gives the camp.

5. *We created for volunteers a team environment–* Volunteer engagement is dependent, in part, on how well volunteers interact, get along and participate on a team. People want to feel like they belong to a community and other volunteers are often the only family volunteers have. Creating a team environment where volunteers get along and work well together helps to create that environment.

6. *We created a culture of trust–* Volunteers need to be able to trust their leadership and are constantly watching to see if their behaviors reflect their words. They want to follow leaders who do what they say, say what they do and are the same regardless of who is around. Credibility is strengthened or lost based on how well a leader demonstrates consistency in their behaviors – both in their personal and professional lives.

7. *We provided clear expectations–* Volunteers need to have a good understanding of their responsibilities and what is expected of them. This is done by providing them with a detailed volunteer job description as well as the training and tools to perform their job. Yet, you must leave room for their creativity that expands ministry.

8. *We recognized volunteers for their worth–* Volunteers like to be acknowledged as a valued part of the camp and a major responsibility of volunteer leadership is to show volunteers care and appreciation for their efforts. This can be done in many different ways, but the key is to send a consistent message of gratitude.

9. *We accepted and used volunteer feedback–* Because volunteers contribute so much of their time, they want to feel like they can participate in the improvement process and that their ideas matter. They want to have a voice in how jobs are performed because they arc often on the front-line and know the best approach to performing job tasks. Volunteers feel valued when a camp actively solicits feedback and incorporates their ideas into how volunteer jobs are carried out. Volunteers have great perspectives and skills that Christian camping needs.

DIRECTION ANTICIPATED IN THE BEGINNING

The first vision was so important because it was the launch of a great calling of the Lord. I remember spending a month alone with my Bible and my dog in a cabin deep in one of Michigan's finest forests. There the Lord guided my thoughts and started a process that is renewed each year. Since the beginning the vision has changed often. What it is today, one could have hardly anticipated. The impact SpringHill has and is making for Christ's Kingdom is reaching around the world: All for God's Glory.

CHAPTER 6

Looking Ahead

"A leader is one who sees more than others see, who sees farther than others see, and who sees before others do."

Leroy Eims - *Be The Leader You were Meant to Be*

Dreams are essential. Dreams can only come to people who stop long enough to think and rest. Dreams come while we sleep. I never have dreams during the heat of the summer; I am too busy thinking about what needs to be done this afternoon to be ready for tonight. I am very near-sighted during the summer.

Some ideas are germinated while at CCCA conferences. We go and see other camps and we begin to ponder how we can implement something similar in our camp. Other dreams are brought to the surface of our minds from reading. Occasionally, I will hear people say, "The Lord told me to do this." Dreams are ideas in need of legs.

I recently read a blog by Dan Rockwell, *The Leadership Freak*, where he talked about thinking out five years and dreaming of where you want to be. But then, he did something very powerful for me. He broke down five years into 260 weeks, and he planted the idea in my mind that now I have to look at each week instead of the five years. I had to begin to plan what I was going to do this week, because next week there would be only 259 weeks left to reach my dream.

Not only did I get my legs, I began to run. It is now been about 4 weeks since I read this idea; I am down to 256 weeks left to accomplish my dream. What is my dream? Retirement. Yep, I will be 65 in five years. Social Security. Medicare. AARP. RV. Down south in winter. Reading. Writing. Consulting with camps. I know my weeks are numbered; I need to begin now getting ready to retire well.

You are on the opposite spectrum of work. You are young and energetic. You see more possibilities ahead than you have time to accomplish. Your mind is all over the place. You have too many ideas and not enough implementation.

When my children were small, they had a push toy that was loaded with brightly colored noisy marbles. As you pushed the toy, the wheels were connected to a mechanism that sent the marbles flying around inside the clear, plastic globe. It was noisy. It was annoying to listen to. It was entertaining to the child and kept him occupied.

I have known directors who sounded like the push toy: noisy and annoying with their ideas. Not that their ideas were annoying, but their talk was annoying. It was all talk. "We are going to do this. I have this great idea. We are going to have this giant capital campaign and raise all the money we need to build this new lodge." Three years later, nothing is built, but these directors are still spouting off that they are going to build something great.

Dan Rockwell also said, "We usually overestimate what we can accomplish in four weeks, and we underestimate what we can accomplish in 260 weeks." I spent 40 years – 2080 weeks -talking about writing a book. It was a dream since my college days. When I finally sat down and was determined to write it, I had the first draft of my first book written in eight weeks – 56 days!

The same holds true with you in your camp. You have the big plan in your head. But you are unable to put legs on it.

Sometimes it is timing. We began drawing the floor plans for a large family life center in 1998. We had a dream. We tried and tried to generate some interest for our plan. We talked, we produced pictures and pamphlets, we promoted. We could not raise a dollar. It wasn't the right time. A few years after our initial dream, a family came forward with a million dollar challenge gift to be matched in three years. We suddenly had legs. It wasn't that our plan was wrong or that we didn't work at promoting it– it simply was the wrong time for the camp to undertake such a project. Today we have a big gym, indoor pool, game areas and lounges for our guests to enjoy.

Sometimes it is a lack of focus. I see this with capital campaigns that are large and expansive. The camp decides to try to do too much with the donations they want to receive. "With the million dollars raised we will build six cabins, one new dining room, and remodel the existing motel rooms," the camp states in its beautiful capital campaign literature. All great projects, but too many projects can confuse people. Stick to one at a time. Donors want to know the exact building their dollars were given towards.

Sometimes it is a lack of clarity of the need. We sometimes focus on just "ministering to more people" in our promotion. Not bad, but not good. People who have the money that can build you new buildings want to know more than just "we want to grow bigger." They want to hear testimonies from Jr. High girls who changed the direction of their lives while at camp last year. Big donors also want to understand how their gifts will provide more financial stability for the camp. I always want to project revenue numbers back to the donors. "When this inn is completed, we will be able to double the income from our retreats. Your gift will be paid back with new business in two years." The donor generated that money from investments he had made earlier in his life, and now he likes hearing how his investment in the camp will provide a pathway to solvency and sustainability into the future. He wants his gift to last for a long time.

Sometimes you just diddle away your ideas in your head. Ouch. You are unprepared to make things happen. Like at the AA meetings you must repeat often, "Hi, I am Joe. I am a diddler. I know it. I waste time thinking too much." Just admitting that you have a track record of great ideas, but little push or drive to implement can help you to change how you operate as a camp director; or it may alert your staff and your board that they are going to need to come alongside you and help you focus on this project alone.

I love this word: **Implementation.** Webster defines it as, "the process of putting a decision or plan into effect; execution." **The process!** Key word in the definition. Not the idea. Not the potential results, but the process.

Rockwell was so right when he lists a timeline and then works backward. It acts like the countdown before an explosion: 10, 9, 8, 7, 6, 5, 4, 3, 2, 1 – explosion or liftoff. Nothing works like pressure. It worked in high school when the term paper was due tomorrow. It works on projects as well. By creating a target date for completion, you have created a countdown. We are building a new dining room and I am saying it will be completed by Labor Day family camp weekend. This is not wishful thinking. This is not a pipe dream. This is real and as the director, I will see that enough manpower is allocated to the project so that it gets done by September 1.

Uncompleted projects usually get defended away with the sorry excuse, "I didn't have enough time!" I don't like that sentence! Wasn't there enough time to check emails, to Facebook insignificant details of your life, and to stand around visiting over lunch? It is not that you don't have time. It is that you don't use your time well.

Implementation is simply focusing on something until the end. Focus is difficult these days. There are always things more interesting and inviting. As I write this, I want to check my Facebook and emails two or three times an hour – just in case someone ate a great meal, and I don't want to miss their picture. Yikes! Successful directors focus and finish and then they relax and enjoy the fruit of their labors. Get those backward and you relax and never finish; you won't last long as the director.

How do you get this focus needed to implement? Practice. Practice on little projects. Plan a flower bed and carry it through until finished. Plan a playground and then build it. Plan building five carpet ball tables– buy the wood and carpet and make sure your maintenance man has the time allocated to build them. Then move on to other larger-scoped projects. Focus becomes a habit because you are getting some results that are beginning to change your camp. Kids are seeing you are accomplishing things. They encourage you with grateful words and that drives you on to the next project.

Plan, push, implement. Well thought-out plans make it easy to implement. Pushing is where it can get hard. Pushing means there will be resistance. There will be shortages of people and money. There will be mistakes that postpone progress. Pushy directors can be seen as bossy and autocratic. Pushy directors will be seen as someone who gets things done.

Learn to push with a smile on your face and with a willingness to jump into the fray and make it happen. Go ahead and get out of your office and get your hands dirty in order to finish on time.

CHAPTER 7

What it Takes to Run a Camp

Henry Ford was asked about his employees.
"None of our men are 'experts.' We have most unfortunately found it necessary to get rid of a man as soon as he thinks himself an expert because no one ever considers himself expert if he really knows his job. A man who knows a job sees so much more to be done than he has done, that he is always pressing forward and never gives an instant of thought to how good and efficient he is. Thinking always ahead, thinking always of trying to do more, brings a state of mind which nothing is impossible. The moment one gets into the 'expert' state of mind a great number of things become impossible."

A director doesn't have to be an expert on all things, but a director needs to be able to do the following:

- **Have understanding:** Maintenance, construction, food service, fund raising, human resources, finances, program, building and grounds.

- **Delegate:** Marketing, promotions, summer camp operations, retreat coordination, bookkeeping, and answering the phones.
- **Do well:** Cry and show empathy, solve problems, write, communicate instructions, motivate staff, clarify grey areas, push projects and provide vision.

The director must show empathy. In order to lead, your staff needs to know you care and have concern for their lives outside of camp. I was weak in this area during my first 20 years. It wasn't until I became of the grandpa-age, that I begin to look at the complete lives of staff. Much of what I do today is walk around and touch base with staff as they work – asking about family, hobbies, and what they are doing this weekend. At the same time, I am asking about and looking at how they are approaching their work load.

The director must be capable of solving problems. It should not come as a surprise to you, but the older generation solves problems. The younger generation is usually unable to find workable solutions to daily irritants. If I see one attribute that will limit the younger director from moving up and expanding her influence, it will be her inability to out-think the daily problems involved in camp life.

Problem solving consumes much of my day; the cooks have problems with ovens, the maintenance staff have problems deciding if they should put more money in repairing one of the pickups, the program people are stuck because of three days of rain. I am there to help them rethink the situation and to move forward with the day. Not only do I solve problems, but I anticipate potential problems. I see potential problems in registration lines. I see problems in the serving lines. I see problems at the zip line. We fix them before they become lasting irritations.

Unsolved problems become potential roadblocks in guest group experiences. Guests love the idea of the zip line, but they don't want to endure the 45 minute wait in the sun in order to get their 45 seconds of whoopee. Problems are not usually understood unless the director is out and about on the grounds. If I stayed at my desk all day, it would never occur to me that there is a line of eight-year-olds standing in the sun waiting for the giant swing, with nothing to do but pick on each other. If I stayed behind the desk, I would never see the food service areas bottle-necked around the salad bar. When I see the problem, I then can reconfigure the set-up so that the line moves smoothly and quickly. I will set a carpet ball table or move a gaga pit next to the swing to occupy the rambunctious boys.

A director must be capable of writing. And no, signing your name to a check does not constitute writing. Writing letters, producing copy for newsletters– putting vision down on paper. Clear writing creates clear plans that people can buy into. Voluminous, superfluous, vague writing consumes too much of the reader's time; make it short and make it sweet. Unless you are writing your personal memoir, say it in less than 250 words and shut up!

A director must give clear instructions. You cannot be mushy and vague. Unclear instructions get unsatisfactory results. Talk with precision. Say exactly what you want accomplished and what the expected results will look like. "Clean up the shop area" usually gets a variety of results depending on who is doing the cleaning. A more exact list will get the exact results the director intended with an assignment. Again, good writing can produce good instructions.

A director must motivate the staff. If you need to understand how much your staff is motivated, leave camp for a few days and see what gets accomplished while you are gone. Motivated staff work just as hard when you are gone as when you are around – they are working to accomplish the mission of the camp. Motivated staff gets the big picture and works toward finishing. Give rewards, increase pay and benefits, provide PTO time, but as Tom Peters says, "Kindness is free," and for camp directors – free is good! Love and care by a director provides a continual flow of serotonin and dopamine– it tells the staff member that all is well with her world. A director needs to be in tune with each staff member's needs for certain types of "strokes."

A director must clarify grey areas. Grey areas are the things and issues not covered in personnel manuals, procedural issues, or the mush that is created when too many people are talking and thinking about something. Sometimes the director must have the fortitude to listen to both sides from staff and make the final call. Right or wrong, a decision is made and the work can go on with clarity.

A director must provide the vision. All staff will have vision. All staff members have an idea of what "they think" the camp should look like or act like. Only the director can create and enforce the culture. Only the director can create the final picture of what camp will look like in five or ten years. He will ask opinions, he will listen to many ideas from staff and boards, but he must paint the final picture. And the director must keep educating and creating fresh vision for the staff to buy into.

So what does it really take to run a camp? You have a degree in business. You worked at a camp through high school and college. You have worked in a church. All good fillers on the resume; resumes are a wonderful tool to show what you should know and what you should have experienced; it is just a poor way of telling us how you have done the job or how you will perform in your next job.

I have received great resumes that *wowed* me. I was ready to hire the person. We have brought the person in for an interview and maybe for a work-alongside weekend together. We want to see the person in action— how she relates to staff, or how she can run a snack bar interacting with guests, or maybe even in the kitchen serving our guests for a weekend. We have seen both a positive and negative discrepancy from what was written on paper and how the potential staff member performs in real life.

Perhaps you are reading this and you aspire to someday take over as the executive director of the camp you are currently working at as a program director, operations manager, or the bookkeeper. It is normal to want to grow into another position. Ask any youth pastor if they want to be a youth pastor until they are 60. It is natural to want to move up.

If you are named the director of the camp before you are 30, I would say that is rare – but not impossible. Camp boards are looking for experience to direct their camp, and at 23 years old, you have not had enough life experiences to qualify. What do you do for the next seven years to prepare yourself for a possible director's position? What skills can you work on that will give you an edge over the other candidates?

I had zero experience in directing a camp when I started at the age of 33. I had worked five years for a Girl Scout camp as the maintenance man. I mowed, cut wood, cleaned buildings, did minor repairs, and even built five cabins. The entire time I worked there, I did what I was told and had very little understanding of the mission of the camp or the organization. However, I was learning something that would become valuable later on as the director. It was not a wasted five years of mowing and cleaning.

When I was hired by Hidden Acres, I came on as the operations manager. I suddenly was thrown into a bigger position that required me to understand food service, housekeeping, maintenance, customer service, and the development of a new camp. At times the director would ask me my opinion and I was asked to sit on the camp board as a staff person and not a voting member. I spent 3 years remodeling the camp house, cleaning, mowing, doing maintenance, cooking and ordering food, meeting with the board, greeting guests on Friday night, providing service, and learning who our churches were and how they functioned as a church.

For eight years I paid my dues. I was college educated – I had an M.A. in English Education. I could have expected to move straight to the top, but instead I did it the old-fashioned way – I earned it! And so must you.

I meet many young directors at CCCA events. I am always interested in how they got their job as the director. I want to know what they did prior to coming to the camp. Some were pastors, some came from the business world, a few were missionaries or involved in an organization like Navigators or Cru. All of them had some type of experience that prepared them to run a camp. Or so they thought.

When you read the chapters written by other directors, you will find a brief history of how they fell into camping. In the 60's and 70's most of us fell into camping by Divine intervention; few of us planned it that way. You will see that Enoch studied at Trinity Divinity School. Tom grew up at the camp, but went to school at Grand Rapids School of the Bible and Music. Brian studied business and psychology and worked for the IRS after college. Dick studied to be an airplane mechanic. I thought I would be a college English professor! But the Lord had other plans. However, we also fell into camping when it was just summer camping or family camp. The retreat business was just getting started. The entire industry was in its infant stage. We were all in small operations that only had summer camps and limited family camps to worry about. Our budgets were small and usually relied on big doses of donor gifts to pay for lights and staff. Today it is different.

Today it is a business. Today it is a big business with sophisticated marketing plans, fund-raising campaigns, development programs and a variety of retreat options that create a busy-ness that would spin most executives' heads. I once read a quote from a CEO that stated, "I would love to hire a successful camp director to work for me, he has learned to keep several projects going at one time and he makes way more decisions per day than I do as the CEO of this large company."

If you are currently a 20-something program director who wants to move up eventually, let me share with you how you can train yourself to be ready when the opportunity arises. It will come, if you build enough skills and disciplines into your life to be ready.

Forget what you learned in college. I hate to be the one to tell you this, but you just spent over $40,000 on not being prepared for camp life. If I had the aspiration to go into camping at 18, I would not waste my time getting a liberal arts degree in English or history! However, you went four years and you still have student loans to remind you of the time spent at your alma mater. A degree might help you to get yourself in the door. It only tells a potential employer you were capable of sticking with something for four years. (Or five, if you were the fun guy at school.)

If you are set on going to a college and you want to prepare for a camp job I would take the following courses: Business writing, shop-woodworking and motor repair, basic architecture classes, theology, basic bookkeeping, marketing classes, public speaking, human resource classes, restaurant and hotel management classes, and newsletter production classes. What would I get my major in? Business? Marketing? Industrial arts? Hotel and restaurant management? All those could be of some value.

However, classroom and reality are miles apart. If you have invested the $40,000 in a B.A., welcome to America, home of the educated, but untrained. It is not your fault you were born into a time that has placed emphasis on class time and books, and not sweat and hand skills.

If I were 23 and working in a camp today, I would want the opportunity to work in every department. I would want to run the dishwasher, help prepare and serve meals and then clean up the kitchen. I would want to run a vacuum, make a bed, clean a toilet, and dust a light fixture. If I were 23 again, I would want to mow lawns, service mowers, cut wood, dig ditches, shingle a roof, help build a wall, and help pull a sewer pump. If I were just getting started in camping I would want to see and work on a budget, look at and understand Quickbooks, and be a part of reviewing the personnel policy manual. I would want to be involved with brochure production, video production, and help manage the website or Facebook page.

See what I mean? You are not ready. But you can be. You can be if you approach each of these unknowns with the right attitude. I love a learner. Give me a learner and a teachable staff person any day over a cocky, know-it-all who is unteachable. Be humble, take instruction, and carry out assigned jobs with excellence. We have three young ladies on our staff today without a day of college;

however, they have become key lead staff by building on their skill set each and every year – they are capable of leading in nearly every department. They can run big equipment (D-7 Cat), cook, serve, do housekeeping, work on the construction crew, produce brochures, run the horse program, and are the three I call on when I want something done now. They are learners, and built their skills to a level of competence that has made them indispensable.

It really is not what you don't know, but it is how you approach what you don't know. Can you get ready in one year? Doubt it. Two? Probably not. Much depends on your desire to learn. Your desire to develop a big picture mentality. It depends on how hungry you are to move into the role of a director. I have seen seasoned camp staff who apply for a director's position and not get the job. Why? Something was lacking. Perhaps they were not multi-skilled. Perhaps they were not people-friendly enough. Perhaps they were a know-it-all and were unteachable.

This I do know. God has designed us for a job. We truly are perfectly and wonderfully made. He gave us innate personality and desires that only we have. I have written earlier, I was born to be the director of a camp. If you are of the Calvinist position, you would say that God already has created a director's position for you. I can believe part of that, but if you are not willing to put in the time and energy to develop a myriad of skills, your dream position as the director of a camp may be frustrating and short-lived.

Today, as the director, I pull very few lift stations. But I know enough about it to make sure a staff person has the tools, help and skills to accomplish the job. I don't cook anymore, but I know the stress that a cook feels about getting a great meal out on time. I don't make beds either, but I do have empathy for the housekeeper, because I know she does a job that is thankless and repetitious. I don't create brochures, but I grasp the amount of time and money it takes to produce a great marketing piece.

The Lord was gracious to me in my early days. I made many mistakes, but I pushed through them. I didn't always treat staff as kindly as I should have; there were days I ran over people to accomplish projects and move the camp along. Those were different days. Today, with the overly connected culture we are currently living in, your faults are going to be magnified 10x what mine were in the 80s. If something happened at work today, rest assured the world will know about it by evening through Facebook or Twitter. You will not be shown the grace I was shown; your sins will be known by supper time.

There is no excuse for not being ready if the perfect camp director's job becomes available. Today, via Amazon and Kindle, you can have 50 or 60 world leaders talking to you through their writings. Podcasts and blogs are available by the boatload. YouTube videos can show you how to fix anything– and I mean anything– your mind could imagine. There is no excuse not to be ready when a position is open.

Learn to speak, learn to write, practice showing empathy, practice giving instructions, learn to fix, and learn to build. Be ready with a resume that matters; a resume that fits a director's position.

CHAPTER 8
Last Man at the Trough

"Create action that is exceptionally alert, externally oriented, relentlessly aimed at winning, making some progress each and every day, and constantly purging low value-added activities— all by always focusing on the heart and not just the mind."

John P. Kotter - *A Sense of Urgency*

You have the title. You have the ability to move and shake and hire and fire and give raises and purchase as you see fit. You are the director; you are in charge.

If you are not careful, you can easily get sucked into believing your title entitles you to special privileges and lessor responsibility. Trust me, I have seen it, I have heard about it, and I have experienced it. Being the boss is more than ordering people around and being the first one to the trough to be fed and praised by guests and donors.

Bottom line, the director is the quarterback of the team; he is not just the coach standing on the sidelines barking out orders. He is not just the offensive coordinator stuck up in the booth high above the playing field analyzing every play. As the quarterback, the director is on the field, calling plays, making changes on the run, encouraging his linemen, and throwing touchdown passes. And in the process of the game, he is taking hits, getting dirty, and feeling the need to work together, shoulder to shoulder with his linemen, tight ends, and running backs– he knows each one is important and necessary in order for him to be successful as the leader.

Coaches are necessary. However, it is the execution that matters. Great ideas, plans, plays, and rules keep the game happening within the boundaries, but it is the execution of the ideas that matters. If there are no touchdowns, then the best laid plans are only dreams and diagrams.

Over the years, I have worked with many camp directors who felt called into this ministry, but have failed to grasp the need to get down and get dirty along with the rest of the team; those directors usually don't last long. It usually takes about 18 months for them to realize they "misheard" their calling into full-time Christian camping.

If you are young or inexperienced, you will not receive an opportunity to become the director of a larger camp that has multiple staff for you to lead. You will probably get the chance to start small in a camp that is in need of some good management and direction. More often than not, you may be asked to direct a ship that has a few loose boards in its side, and is sinking slowly. You are expected to lead and direct this camp out of a hole that has taken years to dig. And, you have to do it alone or with a staff of one or two. If you think you can revive this camp by sitting in the office, think again.

Regardless of how much fun and how meaningful your summer camp experience was to you as a teenager and throughout your college days, when you become the director, camp changes. If you do not anticipate the difference, you will soon be swallowed up with all the details it takes to run the operation, to build the operation, and to oversee the total camp experience.

How did I do it? I juggled. I juggled my many responsibilities. However, I also understood that I was never too smart to dig a hole. Never too important that I couldn't man the dishwasher and relieve the cook from mindless work of scrubbing pots and pans. I was never too dressed up that I could not strip down to a t-shirt and drive the baler or rake the hay. I stood shoulder to shoulder with the rest of the employees; I approached them at their level.

From his book, *Everybody Matters*, Bob Chapman, the owner of Barry-Wehmiller, writes:

"Every single employee is someone's son or someone's daughter. Parents work to offer their children a good life and a good education and to teach them the lessons that will help them grow up to be happy, confident and able to use all the talents they were blessed with. Those parents then hand their children over to a company with the hope the leaders of that company will exercise the same love and care as they have. It is we, the companies, who are now responsible for these precious lives. This is what it means to be a leader. This is what it means to build a strong company. Being a leader is like being a parent, and the company is like a new family to join. One that will care for us like we are their own . . . in sickness and in health. And if we are successful, our people will take on our company's name as a sign of the family to which they are loyal. Those

who work at Barry-Wehmiller talk of their 'love' for the company and each other. They proudly wear the logo or the company's name as if it were their own name. They will defend the company and their colleagues like they were their own flesh and blood. And in the case of nearly every one of these kinds of organizations, the people use the company's name as a very symbol of their own identity."

What is Chapman advocating? Your work should be more heart than head. As the director, you must not think of yourself too highly. Though you have the authority, you also have the responsibility to lead; and leaders eat last. Leaders make sure they show to their staff and volunteers that they too are willing to do the littlest of jobs when it is needed.

Simon Sinek author of *Leaders Eat Last* wrote,

"Those who work hardest to help others succeed will be seen by the group as the leader or the "alpha" of the group. And being the alpha— the strong, supportive one of the group, the one willing to sacrifice time and energy so that others may gain— is a prerequisite for leadership."

When you want the summer staff to follow you: lead. Move ahead of the crowd clearing out obstacles that will interfere with summer staff doing their jobs. Make sure the cabins are set up correctly. Make sure there are adequate bathrooms that are cleaned and maintained. Make sure that there is program equipment needed to carry out the afternoon fun activities. Directors who do ensure that the needed supplies and equipment of a camp exist, are providing a system to build trust.

Directors who want to be followed ensure their full-time staff has the needed tools to succeed. They have the vacuum to clean.

The tools to build. He makes sure that enough staff is hired to complete the job. Successful directors stay late and are the last one home on Saturday night. Successful directors give up holidays to be on call. Great directors wait at the end of the line for benefits and praise from guests – he ensures staff gets their credit first.

Directors who want to be followed always eat last.

CHAPTER 9
Become an Innovator

If you want to build a ship, don't drum up the men to gather wood, divide the work and give orders. Instead, teach them to yearn for the vast and endless sea.

Antoine de St. Exupery

I read. I read a lot. I read at least 30 books a year. I read a variety of materials. I read snippets from USA Today, Huffington Post, Forbes, Money Magazine, Yahoo News, Rush Limbaugh reports, and I listen to farm radio to catch up on grain markets and sowbelly prices. I want to know what is going on in the world from a different perspective. I don't just listen to the Christian perspective.

Though our camps exist in a bubble, we still operate with all the world's influences and behaviors; I want to know what and how the world is viewing business, money, commodities, and personal tastes. I want to know trends. I want to know what is important to the general population today. I need to know so I can plan for tomorrow.

As the director, I have to think larger than the rest of the staff. That is part of my leadership that comes with directing and managing the organization. I like this insight from Earl Nightingale: he discovered a universal truth after reading the simple sentence from Napoleon Hill's book, *Think and Grow Rich*, "*We become what we think about.*"

You know it and I know it, you ain't going to grow rich in camping. The thought of rich and camp is almost an oxymoron! Napoleon Hill was talking about money, but what Earl Nightingale received from this simple sentence is something completely different. He learned that the secret to success was "you had to ruminate on something in order to understand it. You had to read deeper than the headlines to make good decisions, and you had to never stop learning about many things."

How do we apply this to our setting in the Christian camp? Nightingale was looking for the reason why people became successful; he had grown up during the depression and was extremely poor. His impoverished childhood lit his imagination to ask, "Why is someone successful? What did the neighbor do or say or learn that made him successful?" As a camp director, you had better be asking the same question. "What makes other camps successful?" I would hope from reading this book you can catch a glimpse of others who have lived through the life of growing their camps.

I am a big proponent of being curious. Nightingale was curious about why others were successful. That question drove him to read and study and investigate his question. When he read Hill's simple sentence, "We become what we think about," it was an epiphany for him.

I have attended hundreds of CCCA seminars and workshops over the years. Occasionally, I get stuck in round table discussions. Inevitably, there will be one director around the table who will be in a complaining mode. "The economy is against us. We don't have enough business. We are broke. Blah, blah, blah." All woe is me talk! I hate that type of dialogue. I want to stand up and shout, "Why don't you quit your belly-aching and do something about it?" Just as Hill says, they have become what they constantly think about, worry about and dwell on. Their condition paralyzes them from thinking bigger and more productive thoughts.

What are you thinking about today? What thoughts are you pondering? Is it, "Will I make payroll?" Is it, "How will I get more retreats booked? Will I be able to hire another staff person to take some of my load off my plate?" All important questions to ask, but not questions that should be the driving force in your head. Head-talk can become your reality if you are not careful.

Part of why I wanted other successful camp directors to write their personal chapters in this book was to show you that there is no specific way to build and grow a camp. Each director created a vision for the future and then set out to accomplish that goal. Enoch started from scratch and created SpringHill camp from the ground up. Tom inherited a camp that his father started and has created and grown Fort Wilderness into a great organization over the last 25 years. Dick and Brian worked alongside another director for a few years before becoming the director. How did they do it? What are the skills that they had and used that you should emulate? What did they bring into their jobs that gave them favor over the competition? They <u>had</u> success while others floundered, grew old, and became stunted. Both the successful and unsuccessful were living in the same national economy. The successful and the unsuccessful had similar setbacks. What made these guys become leaders that others would follow?

Here is a list that Earl Nightingale wrote as characteristics of innovative people that I read in Chuck Swindoll's book *Come*

Before Winter. When I think of innovative camp leaders, I think of those who, when faced with problems and roadblocks, thought about how to overcome, rethink, and then solve issues that could stop the camp from growing. People who were successful had:

Drive– a high degree of motivation
Courage– tenacity and persistence
Goals– a sense of direction
Knowledge– and a thirst for it
Good health
Honesty– especially intellectual
Optimism
Judgment
Enthusiasm
Chance taking– willingness to risk failure
Dynamism– energy
Enterprise– willing to tackle tough jobs
Persuasion– ability to sell
Outgoingness– friendly
Patient yet impatient– patient with others, yet impatient with the status quo
Adaptability– capable of change
Perfectionism– seek to achieve excellence
Humor– ability to laugh at self and others
Versatility– broad interests and skills
Curiosity– interested in people and things
Individualism– self-esteem and self-sufficiency
Realism/idealism– occupied by reality but guided by ideals
Imagination– seeking new ideas, combinations, and relationships
Communication– articulate
Receptive– alert

Wow! That is some list. And as I have read biographies of great people who did great things, I think the list is universal. It was true with the Wright brothers, it was true with President Teddy Roosevelt, it was true Cyrus the Great, and it is true with Billy Graham. It is true with Enoch Olson and Brian Ogne and Tom Robertson and Dick Angelo. It can be true with you.

You can't just read one book and then your mind will be changed. Camps are funny critters. We are not a pure business, but we have to act like one. We are not a pure ministry, because we earn income and do not rely on 100% donations; we are not the local church that takes up offerings to fulfill the budget. We are caught in the middle. Caught might not be the right word – perhaps we "get" to be in the middle. We get to earn money with our hard work and service to groups. We get to minister to junior high campers who see their lives full of more questions than answers. We get to work alongside families training and developing their sons and daughters to be leaders.

If you have tried to read a book on how to be a successful business, say by reading, *Amaze Every Customer Every Time* by Shep Hyken, you would learn some principles on customer service and treating your guests like family, but Ace hardware doesn't have 10-year-old campers to contend with. You could read Danny Meyer's, *Setting the Table* to learn about the food service industry and outlandish customer service, but Danny has never had to feed 300 fourth and fifth graders on a budget of $1.50 per meal. You could read Joseph Michelli's book, *The New Gold Standard*, and learn about all the great things Ritz Carlton does to ensure customer loyalty, but Ritz Carlton has not seen your 3 inch plastic coated mattress stuck in a cabin that is 200 yards from the nearest bathroom. (I highly recommend all these books).

But here is what happens over time. Read enough, study enough and pretty soon your brain begins to think like the different writers. Pretty soon you begin to understand how guests feel about awkward and clumsy systems and procedures in your operation. Do you think that people are staying away from your camp because you are not a nice enough guy? Being a nice guy only counts if you are a politician. Being nice doesn't take the place of poor service, poor procedures, and poor facilities. Read enough stories about successful businesses and pretty soon you will see your shortcomings and become committed to changing things.

Our resources are limited at camp. I know of very few camps that are financially "loaded." Most camps just get by. Some only get by because they have cut their services down to bare-bones and meager rations. I know those camps! I have been to them, and quite frankly, they are depressing as you look at the facilities from an outsider's point of view. However, I also know these depressing facilities are usually managed and operated by great people who love the Lord. Their intent is of the highest value – they want boys and girls to come to know Christ while on their property. That is their mission and that is why they endure.

Earl Nightingale and even Earl Taylor are old guys; Nightingale was born in 1921 and died in 1986. They are both old geezers in the eyes of the 20-something up and coming new director. Over-the-hillers. AARPers. Out-of-touch seniors. What Nightingale wrote and saw as universal principles were principles that I used in developing the camp. So did Enoch, so did Tom, so did Dick, so did Brian.

If you are looking for a new program to kick start your life as a director, you are not going to find it. If you are looking for an angle or gimmick or a new skill to ensure your success, you probably won't arrive there. However, if you want to work on your own personal character, work on the attributes previously mentioned and immerse yourself in developing the person who will exemplify all the attributes listed in Nightingale's list; then there is a great chance you will be successful in moving your camp forward to growth and sustainability. Because guess what? Your camp will never outgrow you as the leader. It will not become something you are not. It will not become bigger than you allow it.

Every writer in this book has their story. I have been to all of their camps. I have seen and heard of their humble beginnings. I have seen how they improvised with something home-made until something better could be purchased. I saw pictures of their original cabins and wondered, "How did they get anyone to stay in such primitive housing?" I saw where they cooked out of a tent-kitchen until they could afford something with real walls. Trust me, these directors were innovative. They had more problems than you may ever face, but they overcame problems with solutions— solutions that got them through one more summer until they had enough time to build something permanent. You will see that none of them started with "perfect." They all started with ideas, dreams, and a handful of faithful donors and board members who believed in the mission of the camp. They started with an attitude of persistence and grit; they had an iron will which allowed them to stick with it long enough to finally enjoy the fruits of their labors.

Iron will. The Urban Dictionary definition says, *"A burning determination that cannot be stopped or hindered by anything; willing to do anything to get a desired outcome; extremely resilient."*

Iron will does not mean stupid. It does not mean you bury your head in the sand and not understand when you should fold up your tent and go elsewhere. It doesn't mean you will succeed if you keep at something long enough.

I met a young man at a camp some time ago, who was carrying on the dream of his father who had started a camp in the 1970's. The initial mission of the camp was excellent: it was to be a training grounds for young men. It was to be a summer camp. This young director was trying to accomplish the original goals from 40 years ago without the needed skills, resources, and backing from any churches, and his dad lived two states away. It was the first time I ever had to tell someone, "Give it up. It is not going to happen at your camp." This director had iron will. He would not give up. His was stupid iron will. His was misguided iron will.

If you are new at a camp that is facing challenges, you need iron will. If you are in need of more money, more time, and in need of a very handy maintenance man to relieve you of late night hours fixing furnaces and ovens – you need iron will.

You attend the sectional conferences at large camps and wonder how they got to this point– lots of nice buildings, plenty of staff, a maintenance shed with bobcats and mowers and backhoes, and a weekend schedule that is busting at the seams, wishing your camp had the same. You are wondering if you can ever bring your camp up to this level. What does it take? **Iron will focused on the right things.** Not all things, but the right things that enable the camp to grow. Not all activities are the right activities. Not all activities add value to the camp. Not all activities add to the financial bottom line of the camp.

I am a facilities/building guy. Other directors refer to me as Earl the builder. You will read of other directors who are program oriented. Some will tell you how they built their camp by building a strong team around them. Each has worked. Each is partially applicable to you and your camp. Read carefully, but implement slowly. What we are pouring out in this book took us all 20 and 30 years to accomplish. Take one idea and implement it. Come back and work a second idea. Then a third. You get the idea. As you read this book, create a top 10 list of great things to try and then write it down on the inside of the cover. Mark up the book. Come back to it when you are facing a wall of despair.

Take one of those many things that keep dragging you under and search for a creative way to solve the problem. And don't quit until it's done – then start again on the next hurdle.

CHAPTER 10
My Story - Brian Ogne

Brian led in Christian camping for 40 years; his constant positive attitude and enthusiasm have been received by countless other directors throughout CCCA in workshops and personal visits. I always considered Brian as the perfect camp cheerleader and fundraiser.
He loves people. brianogne@elknet.net

(Author's Note)

Barb and I served as home missionaries in Christian camping from May 1969 through May 2009.

After a commissioning service in our home church, Bethel Community Church in Chicago, we arrived at our Christian camp assignment at Camp Willabay in Williams Bay, Wisconsin, (the predecessor of Timber-lee Christian Center) with a nine-month-old son and an assignment to be the director of camping. I was the fourth full-time staff member at Willabay. Our executive director, foodservice director, and maintenance director were there as the team.

Camp Willabay, an Evangelical Free Church camp, started in 1946 and has a great heritage of serving the Christian camps in southeastern Wisconsin and northern Illinois. Camp Willabay had as its primary purpose, "To present Jesus Christ as Savior and Lord and to reveal His embracing love to every boy and girl and man and woman that comes on the grounds." This was my "calling" all 40 years.

There were many hats that we had to have in those early years. Most of mine were in the following areas: developing programs, registering and hosting guests, preparing brochures, visiting churches for promotions, raising support, promotion and recruitment of staff and campers, working with the board, planning fundraising events, community relations, and training staff, etc. We gathered the best and the brightest we could find from our local colleges, churches, and community volunteers. These were the daily responsibilities of this position as director of camping.

After three years at Camp Willabay, God gave us a huge vision of a much bigger facility. In 1972, we bought a 550 acre, fully developed camp 20 miles north of Willabay that was owned by the Hull House Association of Chicago. We named it Timber-lee Christian Center. The ministry grew, almost doubling in the first two years. God was so faithful and evident to us as we trusted Him and received guidance daily through encouragement, support, and God's Word. I assumed the responsibility in 1972 of director of camping at Timber-lee Christian Center and kept that role through 1979.

In 1980, I assumed the role of executive director and eventually president of Timber-lee Ministries. Over those years, our board of directors was strong in leadership, counsel, and support. We grew from a budget of $500,000 to over $4 million annually.

We moved from 35 acres at Willabay to 550 acres at Timber-lee. From four full-time staff to 50 full-time staff. From 2,000 guests to 65,000 guests on the grounds each year. From hundreds of spiritual decisions to thousands of spiritual decisions each year. From accommodating 110 campers in tents and small cabins to 850 guests in comfortable indoor lodging. From 18 buildings at Willabay to eventually 50+ buildings at Timber-lee.

Those 40 years gave Barb and me great joy and blessing as we have seen many staff return to share that they are going on to full-time Christian service, and to find over 100 couples who met at Timber-lee moved on in their relationships to marry as a result of serving on summer staff. We developed a full RV campground, a Saddle Horn Ranch horse program which grew from 15 horses at Willabay to over 50 horses, and a science education center.

God provided for us in the latter years an additional 1000 acres in the Upper Peninsula of Michigan so we could expand our wilderness program. In the last few years, after having it over eight years, we were able to sell it for a huge return on the investment allowing us to do major improvements on our present site at Timber-lee.

God richly provided as we trusted Him for spiritual results, safety, financial support and growth.

My greatest joy aside from this opportunity to serve the Lord through our Christian camping ministries at Willabay and Timber-lee was my involvement in CCI, now CCCA and also in CCI/Worldwide. During these years, I have attended Christian camping conferences as an attendee, as a workshop leader and as an elected officer.

I attended the Wisconsin Sectional of CCI and the Midwest Regional Conventions, serving as an officer in Wisconsin and chairman of the region for a number of years. I also had the privilege of serving as treasurer of the USA Board of Directors for two terms and the President of the National Board for a term. It allowed me to "rub shoulders" and learn from great men and women who have leadership roles in our CCI/USA Christian camping movement.

Attending National Conventions with the opportunity to teach seminars, lead workshops, and enjoy the general session speakers gave me a wonderful overview of the big picture of Christian camping and the opportunity to fellowship with other great camping leaders whose stories I will never forget. I have kept records, notebooks, seminar notes, personal notes and many conference convention tapes and they have become my resources and counsel for all my years in ministry in Christian camping and beyond.

Serving on the USA Board as President, I was allowed to represent USA at the international convention of CCI/Worldwide. Seeing the international picture of Christian camping was so rewarding. As Chairman of the international Council for a term, I was able to preside over the 15 countries that made up our CCI/Worldwide Association. Making friends worldwide and participating in some national conventions in four different countries as the speaker was so rewarding.

I have had the opportunity to mentor many young staff encouraging them in their training and leadership in camping. Many have followed that and at least six have become camp directors over the years serving in Christian camps around the United States and the world. It's been a great honor and privilege to see the Lord allow me to share in their lives and see them flourish.

I have collected, created, and taught many workshops and seminars at Christian camping events. Much of what I have used in my training of others is tested and proven effective. Here are some outlines I have used.

Workshop 1– *Ten principles that have guided me over 40 years of leadership in Christian camping.*

1. **Attitude … Integrity**
   a) Chuck Swindoll's definition of attitude is my favorite. Swindoll says, "The longer I live, the more I realize the impact of attitude on life. Attitude to me, is more important than facts, the past, education, money, circumstances, failures, successes, and what other people think or say or do. It is more important than appearance, giftedness or skill. It will make or break a company, a church, a home. The remarkable thing is, we have a choice every day regarding the attitude we will embrace for that day. We cannot change our past…we cannot change the fact that people will act in a certain way… we cannot change the inevitable. That only thing we can change is our attitude. I am convinced that life is 10% what happens to me and 90% how I react to it. And so it is with you also. We are all in charge of our own attitudes."
   b) Strive for complete integrity in business practices and in your life.
   c) Trust God… He is faithful – I Chronicles 28:20 – Be strong and courageous and get to work. Don't be frightened by the size of the task, for the Lord my God is with you; He will not forsake you. He will see to it that everything is finished correctly.

2. **Build People and Make Them Successful:**
   a) Clear position descriptions

b) Hire slower, fire faster.

c) Always maintain clear lines of authority from top to bottom in your staffing.

d) Review and evaluation of staff

e) Deal fairly with discipline and removal.

f) Build long-term relationships.

g) Employer satisfaction…dollars are not first on the list of what employees want.

h) Hire a human resources director early who can formulate compensation packages, insurance, and staff training programs.

3. **Utilize Your Uniqueness**

a) Knowing your strengths and weaknesses are an essential part of the process. When you know who you are, you can be comfortable making decisions about what you want to do and where.

b) Understand social styles.

c) No social style is wrong but people are grouped into four categories in the way I learned which would be driver, analytical, amiable, and expressive. Some believe that a type A personality is the only kind that can be a leader but any of these four make great leaders if they understand their social style and how it relates to the other employees. Understanding your staff and family is very beneficial. I recommend the book, *Dancing with Porcupines,* by Bob Phillips.

4. **Decide, Delegate, Disappear**

   a) Learn the art of delegation sooner.

   b) Don't be a bottle neck.

   c) The secret to failure is trying to please everybody.

   d) Don't get too focused on internal problems or bureaucracy.

   e) Watch those legal issues.

5. **You Are the KEEPER OF THE VISION:**

   a) You are the holder of the vision. Carry it and share it with others.

   b) Know:

   – Where are we going?

   – Who is going along with us?

   – What are we good at as we go along?

   – Who knows?

6. **Own Your Mission Statement**

   a) Taking time to do a mission statement and set measurable goals is crucial to any business or in your personal life.

   b) Write it out, memorize it, make what we call an "elevator statement" and live it.

   c) Customer service.

   d) At times, we are changing methods but not changing our mission.

7. **Learn How to Raise Money**

   a) Understand the four principles of funding your ministry…

   – People give money because they want to.

- People don't give unless they are asked.
- People give money to people... to make a change for the good.
- People give money to success, not to distress.

b) Key is building relationships.

c) Thank your donors or contributors more often.

d) Best fundraising is person to person.

e) Talk vision not need.

8. **Understand Boards and Marketing:**

a) Get the board in your boat, but don't give them the oars.

b) Know your board is behind you, but not too far behind.

c) Be more aggressive in marketing. For camp, our motto was, "An empty bed is a ministry lost."

9. **Seek Older, Wiser Counsel Often**

a) Work with fellow camping leaders whom you trust and admire.

b) Don't be afraid to hire consultants.

c) Attend CCCA conferences. Listen, learn, and teach.

10. **Don't Forget Your Family:**

a) Help your mate find joy and purpose in her life.

b) Take time for your kids (vacations, school meetings, sports, hobbies, and responsibilities).

c) Enjoy sunsets together.

d) Do more singing ... laugh out loud more.

e) List God's miracles in your life and list times of awe.

f) John Dresser's book, *If I Were Starting my Family Again*:

- I would love my wife more

- I would be a better listener

- I would be more encouraging

- I would seek to develop feelings of belonging

- I would seek to share God more intimately

Workshop 2– *Ten things I recommend to new, young camp directors going into their first camp experience.*

1. A clear position description: Be sure that your responsibilities, your limits and to whom you are responsible are clearly defined.

2. Salary: Be sure there is a clear understanding of your salary, benefits, time off, lines of authority and whether your spouse will be able to be employed on an hourly basis.

3. Development: One of the first responsibilities you will have is to begin a major listing of names and addresses of potential donors. This includes individuals, churches, businesses, friends and family.

4. Business operations: Develop a budget and determine what percentage you will raise through operations income and what percentage will be gifts income, establish a bank account, and learn all the IRS rules and requirements to run a 501c# corporation. Get a board member or volunteer to serve as treasurer. Keep accurate books.

5. Promotion and marketing: Develop a master plan for the entire year, programming out the activities your organization will sponsor and others that will be rentals. Start

utilizing your uniqueness and fill your beds as fast as you can with income-producing programs and rentals.

6. Staffing: Work on volunteers and begin hiring as available. Consider the first person you hire an addition to yourself and someone who will be fundraising. Consider your standard maintenance, food service, and program people.

7. Community involvement: Get involved by getting to the local citizens and leaders.

8. CCCA: Get involved immediately in the state sectional and attend national conventions where you will gain insight and practical knowledge on camping skills.

9. Develop a statement of mission and a logo.

10. Develop a master plan: Once you get a handle on the first year you will be able to develop some long range and short range plans (1-2 years, 3-5 years) for future growth that can be presented to your board.

Workshop 3- *To be the most effective as executive director:*

1. Spend more time in church mission dollar cultivation.

2. Thanking big donors

3. Raising big gifts for capital campaigns.

4. Planning the future with long range plans and drawings.

5. Sharpening the focus of the ministry.

6. Urban outreach support dollars.

7. Leadership development of staff and hiring new key staff on a regular basis.

8. Filling your beds year around.

9. Organizing my records.

10. Community involvement.

Workshop 4- *Ten principles under which I desire our summer staff to operate*

1. Care.
2. Have a goal of changed lives.
3. Excellence... go for it!
4. Camp is for the campers and the staff.
5. Camp is a tool, not a toy.
6. We must maintain a positive motivation.
7. Be versatile and flexible.
8. Set goals and reach them.
9. Never underestimate the power of prayer.
10. Always be aware of the enemy.

Workshop 5- *20 tips that will keep you both out of trouble*

Tips to Christian camp board members and CEO's- suggested by Bob Kobielush, former president of CCCA/USA

1. Determine that the key function of the board is to make good decisions. Everything else is either preparation for those decisions or implementation thereof.
2. A board's biggest and most important decision is to select the right person to be the CEO.
3. If a board member feels the CEO is not the right person for the job, they must share this concern with the board chair, who then has the responsibility to proceed appropriately with the rest of the board. If, over a period of time, you feel the situation does not improve, and the board feels contrary, you should resign.
4. Annually the CEO must be evaluated both on performance and attitude and corresponding appropriate

decisions/actions should take place which include considerations with regard to remuneration/benefits.

5. The CEO must willingly submit to the authority of the board, but not at the expense of continuing to contribute to the decision-making process and positive implementation.

6. Each year the board members and the CEO should re-commit themselves to the tasks of being in leadership, within the established guidelines, or be willing to resign.

7. If the decision making process is impaired, for whatever reason, address the core issues with the board and plan for changes. If the board disagrees you may have come to a point where your ministry can be done more effectively elsewhere.

8. Don't confuse diversity of opinion and perspective as negative. Use it as a base for building a positive complete ministry.

9. Feel positive and honored by the role you play in this organization, or move on.

10. If you feel your camp/conference ministry would be negatively affected, in a significant way, by your lack of commitment or action with regard to Biblical principles, and understood by your supporting constituency, resign.

11. Understand that Christian camp/conference ministry is a complex and demanding, but extraordinarily worthwhile Christian venture.

12. At least 50% of your board meetings should be held at your camp/conference center.

13. Board meetings should be conducted in an appropriate business atmosphere (setting and amenities) so the environment promotes good discussion and decision making.

14. Always open board meetings with prayer, some type of devotional and a time for members to express themselves with regard to personal need or joy. God's work done by God's people, in God's way is critical to Christian camp/conference ministries.

15. Remember, adjourned is adjourned. While a board member has responsibility and influence for and in the organization 24 hours a day, 7 days a week, their authority, as a board member, only exists within the meeting, and one can only act on behalf of the board when such authority has be specifically delegated. All else comes under the direct authority of the person hired to direct/manage the camp/conference.

16. To conduct a solvent camp/conference ministry, one must make good decisions about solvency and ministry AND both must be seen as spiritual exercises.

17. Gain a reputation for taking good physical and spiritual care of guests/campers and staff alike, or consider yourself a failure in all you do.

18. Remember, Christian shoddy is still shoddy.

19. In addition to all else, be a financial contributor to your camp/conference.

20. To God be the glory, having a sense that He is using you for His purpose.

CHAPTER 11
Shake It Up

Multipliers are genius makers. Everyone around them gets smarter and more capable. People may not become geniuses in a traditional sense, but Multipliers invoke each person's unique intelligence and create an atmosphere of genius— innovation, productive effort, and collective intelligence.

Liz Wiseman - *Multipliers: How the Best Leaders Make Everyone Smarter*

Staff hates this. They will fight you. They will accuse you of losing part of your thinking capabilities. However, you must shake it up occasionally for the sake of the long-term health of the camp.

Peter Drucker states:

"The disturbing element in an organization consists of one or more leaders who prod people to develop, improve, innovate, and sustain the spirit of the organization. They often disturb the status quo by pursuing destabilizing, systematic innovation, which is essential to achieving and sustaining a spirit of performance....Those executives who provide the sustaining spirit for an organization are forever

91

watchful for bureaucratic tendencies allowing people to drift into repetitive routines and lose focus on primary results." Joseph A. Maciariello: *A Year with Peter Drucker: 52 Weeks of Coaching for Leadership Effectiveness*

As soon as your staff around you begins to become comfortable and content, it is time to shake it up. Delete programs, flush out obscure information gathering routines, rearrange positions and reassign staff to new positions and responsibilities.

"Abandonment of any program is difficult for a nonprofit organization because of the strong belief in the righteousness of its cause. It is sometimes difficult for a for-profit organization to abandon a program because the program may represent an investment by the people who introduced it and who nursed it along. Beware of commitment to ego as an excuse for maintaining the status quo." Joseph A. Maciariello: *A Year with Peter Drucker: 52 Weeks of Coaching for Leadership Effectiveness*

The act of shaking up the system forces staff to move from routine into the unknown – where their performance goes up and their effectiveness and efficiencies increase.

Directors who are capable of this with regularity will provide a camp with fresh vision that the staff has to keep working towards. Staff who are allowed to do their same jobs continuously, begin to create the silo mentality that says, "I only do this job and expect no more from me."

However, when you begin to do this, you had better know enough and have spent enough time understanding people's gifts and understand the systems that are currently in place.

Let me give you an example. Not all reports are of value. Some reports were part of the camp culture of reporting noses and plates and beds. Once an office worker had the ability to create a report of graphs and charts full of circles, and pie shapes designated as plates or noses or beds, graphic charts became a part of the reporting process. However, not all charts are necessary. Not all charts meet the need of what a director needs to know. Sometimes, you must force staff to switch their information systems to communicate what you need now, and not what was needed 15 years ago. It is busy work creating charts and graphs; it is fun work for staff, but it produces no information that is even needed.

Sometimes it means you need to pull a particular responsibility away from one staff person who is failing on accomplishing the job assigned, and give it to someone else who is better suited to fulfill the job responsibility.

Tip-toeing around staff's feelings is debilitating; it sucks the life out of me. I have taken staff who were doing just average at one job and completely reassigned them to an entirely different part of the camp; they resisted at first, but usually once they settle in, they go from good to great. This is not done without many months of assessment and evaluation on the director's part. It is done by giving certain assignments or projects and watching how the staff handles the particulars of the project. This takes time on the director's part to go through certain steps of evaluation.

My first published magazine article in 1984 was titled, *Make it Fresh, Move Around*; it was a how-to article for bow hunters. I am still preaching the same sermon after all these years – only now I am preaching to the staff! Shake it up!

CHAPTER 12

Design Matters

There is a wonderful story of a group of American car executives who went to Japan to see a Japanese assembly line. At the end of the line, the doors were put on the hinges, the same as in America. But something was missing. In the United States, a line worker would take a rubber mallet and tap the edges of the door to ensure that it fit perfectly. In Japan, that job didn't seem to exist. Confused, the American auto executives asked at what point they made sure the door fit perfectly. Their Japanese guide looked at them and smiled sheepishly. "We make sure it fits when we design it." In the Japanese auto plant, they didn't examine the problem and accumulate data to figure out the best solution— they engineered the outcome they wanted from the beginning. If they didn't achieve their desired outcome, they understood it was because of a decision they made at the start of the process.

Simon Sinek- *Start with Why: How Great Leaders Inspire Everyone to Take Action*

Perfect design creates near-perfect results. Haphazard design creates havoc and disillusionment.

What makes a piece of furniture comfortable? What makes it uncomfortable or unsafe to rock in? Design. Give me a comfortable chair any day over a modern, fancy chair that is made only to be seen and not sat in. They are sitting in parlors and formal dining rooms that no one is allowed to go into unless a special occasion is happening: twice each year. Give me the over-stuffed La-Z-Boy that is stuck out of the way in the family room. It feels good to my bones. I can kick back, lean back, and enjoy my sit.

Camps are designed. Culture is designed. Personal interactions are designed. It is a matter of who does the designing. Successful camp directors take charge of the design of all functions, all facilities and promote the design.

What am I saying?

Did I have the breadth and scope of design issues necessary as a young director? No. But I did ensure that what was designed was mine. Granted, I had the blessing of beginning my career at a camp that was only six years old; there was nothing designed except for a master plan. There was no culture. There was no systems. There was no one saying, "We have never done it that way before." I was able to create, manage, and develop as I saw fit.

Things will be different if you are the new director to an old camp. The die has been cast. There are traditions, systems, and a culture firmly rooted in place. With this, you are caught in the middle, wanting to change the camp to fit you and your personality. You may have to wait.

You may have to wait until you grasp the history of the camp. You are going to have to wait until you understand what traditions have value, and what traditions are valueless. You may have to wait until you catch the internal flavor of how the current staff, whom you will be working with, views their past and their systems and the traditions that they have lived with under the former director.

Occasionally, new/young directors are given the opportunity to take a flourishing, sustainable, growing camp and take it on to a higher level; this usually occurs when a long-standing director retires and the new director is promoted from within. However, for most young directors, you must start with a smaller, older, perhaps even a struggling camp; you have to prove yourself and gain knowledge and experience before you get invited to direct a large multi-faceted camp.

I have seen it often. I have seen highly gifted, first-time directors who are full of energy and ideas wash up within two years of service. Many leave the camping ministry, disheartened, discouraged and having decided to never "do camping" again. The love of camping that they had developed as a camper and a summer staffer quickly dissolved into disillusionment and weariness.

You are reading this book because you are either so newly into Christian camping that you have no idea what you are doing, or you have reached a barrier that finally is forcing you to look beyond your own personal gifts and talents for advice and direction. What you thought was going to be a fun, exciting, relational job has turned into a dead-end marathon, full of traditions that you must fight against every day. You are finding a staff who is content with their C- performance. You are finding that your current facilities are no longer adequate or acceptable for today's retreaters. You are stuck and need a plan.

I personally love design. Great design. Design that functions well and is cost effective. Design that allows all systems to work together seamlessly. Our bodies work that way. It was perfectly designed by The Creator to function together. The brain sends signals to the stomach and the stomach functions, so that the blood will receive the nutrients that it needs. When the body stops functioning correctly, it is called sickness or disease; organs are working against each other rather than for each other.

If you could simplify what makes up a camp you could probably break it down into five different departments: administration, food service, program, maintenance, and housekeeping. These are simplistic titles of different departments. Each department has sub-categories. Administration could cover fund-raising, marketing and promotions, registrations, bookkeeping, and staff development. Each of these could be broken down even further.

Each position or job description must fit together into something that works and functions without disruptions and inconsistencies. It must be designed well. The retreat registrar must have a system that tells the housekeepers which group is using which building at what time and their special needs. If the system fails, we create opportunities for guests to be unhappy and unsatisfied with their camping experience at our camp; they might look elsewhere for next year's retreat.

I will not tell you how we do our camp; our systems work for our camp, but may not work for yours. Ours systems were designed so that they work with our current staff. Remove one key staff person from the equation and the system will need to be re-worked. If the registrar leaves her job, then it will take some time and effort in creating new systems to fit the style and gifts of the new registrar. We would not scrap all systems– the CampBrain computer program will stay the same, but minor details will change and be adapted. Accept and expect it.

Let me give you an example. We had a long-time retreat registrar who was preparing to retire from the position a few years back.

She was old school in that she had created a long-hand calendar to keep track of the upcoming retreats– pencil and paper. We hired a 25-year-old to replace her. Due to the complexity of understanding the retreat business, they were able to work alongside each other for about three years with the older one gradually releasing responsibilities piece by piece. The young one was adamant that she would convert all retreat information to a computer program that would be easier to administer; five years later she is still using the pencil and paper method. But here is the rest of the story.

She did take over the position of retreat registrar, but she has taken the responsibility to a higher level. She did not throw out something completely that was designed over time by her predecessor. There was merit in the pencil and paper system; it worked and it was efficient. However, she has purposely designed additional methods to communicate to the rest of the staff who are needing the information that she has assimilated from emails and talking to church retreat coordinators. Was her first worksheet she handed out to staff perfect? No. But over time she kept listening, kept watching where staff were dropping the ball in their preparation for a retreat group and redesigned little aspects and key points to the information sheet that our guest service and program staff needed to prepare properly.

If you are new to camping, start slow designing your new and improved systems. You need at least three years to grasp and understand. If the house is on fire or the foundation is crumbling, you might not have a three year window; you must react and create systems immediately to stop the bleeding. You will need to quickly do camp triage within the first month.

If you have a healthy camp that you have inherited, I would spend the first year listening and changing very little. If changes are made, it probably should be talked out extensively with staff. If you are coming from another camp, your new staff doesn't want to hear you say, "At my old camp we did such and such." They don't care! Your old camp *ain't* their camp!

I have seen pastor after pastor begin their time at a new church with new ideas, new programs, new, new, new. And they are met with stubbornness, traditions, and old blue-haired ladies that could stare a hole through a wall; they shall not be moved. The fight is on, and often, the pastor suddenly feels called to another church. The same thing happens at camps.

Learn to ask why? And learn to ask why gently, without an attitude. "Help me understand why we always serve this type of cinnamon rolls every Saturday? Help me understand why the wilderness program always takes a canoe trip down the river on Thursday? Help me know why we always build cabins with a loft?" Get the tone?

It is not the probing that destroys relationship with staff, it is the tone. It is the, "I know more than you do, so get over it, bucko, and do it my way," tone.

Slowly, you will earn the right to redesign your camp. Slowly, you can turn stale traditions into marketable exclamation points. Slowly, you can retrain staff to see their camp and their work through your eyes.

CHAPTER 13
The Micawber Principle
... *something will show up!*

First, it's what one does that counts. Good intentions, a positive attitude, and enormous enthusiasm are not enough. Thoughts don't even matter. What counts is the physical action one takes, right here in the tangible world. Second, getting things right most of the time is good enough. The things that don't come out well are just part of the overhead: the cost of doing business, of taking risks, of uncontrollable external confusion, of coping with events that are sometimes one step ahead of your best efforts; of being alive. As by-products of your advancement forward, accept that less-than-perfect events are going to happen. Three steps forward and one step back is the way it goes. Third, remember that most people don't fail by making overt mistakes. They fail because they don't take action. If you fall into this category, prepare to change your ways.

Sam Carpenter– *Work the System: The Simple Mechanics of Making More and Working Less*

Some directors are like Wilkins Micawber, a Dickens character in his book *David Copperfield*, whose life mantra and perspective were "something will show up." Wilkins is correct to a degree, "something" will turn up, but what?

Micawber lived in hopeful expectation. He never was sure of what or how good things were going to come about, but he was content in letting them come to him "as they pleased." He didn't work towards any particular results, but instead was content to let the chips fall as they willed. Listen to Micawber talk:

> "Annual income twenty pounds, annual expenditure nineteen pounds nineteen and six, result happiness. Annual income twenty pounds, annual expenditure twenty pounds nought and six, result misery."

Many camps understand this concept of happiness when there is money in the bank, and misery when we are broke: we have all experienced both sides of the ledger.

Much of camp work aims toward our mission, usually something like "to know Christ and to make Him known." Our work leads to ministry opportunities either during our summer camps or our retreat season. We plan all winter so that our summers will help populate Heaven: we expect results.

However, much of what a camp is capable of accomplishing depends on creating a good financial plan. There has to be enough business entering camp to pay the bills, pay the staff, keep the camp updated, and provide resources for those in the trenches of summer camp. Broken down facilities and poorly paid personnel eventually lead to empty beds and closed down camps.

Earning more than you spend works for Micawber and it must work for you. The secret is to get the income up to a level that pays the bills and allows for constant updates and remodels. It is not a fatalistic approach. It is a direct approach that forces all staff to work hard to accomplish.

Using the Micawber principle, "something will show up and save us," usually doesn't happen. Like it or not, healthy camp finances boil down to this: have you filled enough beds and produced enough plates of food? When you have to rely on a larger percentage of your operating budget coming from donations, you lose control and are at the mercy of both the donor's ability to give and in a larger context, the total economy of the state you live in.

A simple metric that can show you if you are moving in the right direction would be to determine the percentage of gift income to earned income for your general fund. When we first began, we were operating with a 55% to 45% split- with earned income being the larger number. Over the years of building the business, we eventually grew to 75% earned income. A few years later we were up to 90%. Today we are over 95%. Typically, it is not where you are currently standing that matters, but whether you have been increasing your earned income each year.

I worked with a camp in Texas a few years ago. When I arrived at the camp, I was shocked at how beautiful the buildings were in comparison to the impression I had received by looking at their website. They had it all as a camp: plenty of nice comfortable beds, great meeting spaces, a beautiful dining room, but nobody could tell that from their website; they needed to improve their marketing by redesigning their website. Once a new website was built, their business improved dramatically. People were finally able to see what a great camp it was by going online. Consequently, church retreat coordinators took the next step and came to the camp where they found that the website pictures matched reality: they could now book with confidence. The director and his wife stopped using the Micawber principle and did something about their financial condition: they have a great website now.

When you try to apply the Micawber principle to your camp, you are really approaching the business with a foreboding perspective: "If the Lord wants us to grow and prosper, he will send us the groups and we will become a success." This statement sounds a bit simple and pious, but I have heard different versions of it many times. Some sound like this: "If the board would let us do this." "If our churches would only start using us." "If we just could convince our pastors to talk about us more from the pulpit." Directors who use the "if" word drive me crazy.

Guess what. It isn't anybody's fault or responsibility to grow the business but yours! You, as the director, must carry the entire load of responsibility. Saying, "The Lord will provide," only gives you an easy escape that allows you to stop driving the business. When you let excuses drive, you end up sitting in the back seat with Miss Daisy and you will continue to be at the mercy of whatever you decide is your problem.

How do you move from the back seat to the front? Owning the problem is the start. Understanding that it is your job, your responsibility to make the camp work is the first step. Not only work, but thrive and grow. The statement you have read is correct: if you are not moving forward, you are moving backward, there is no neutral.

This is not about your budget. Your budget means very little in how you operate the camp. The budget actually can work against your mind. I have heard directors state, "I wrote it down in the budget to earn $500,000 in retreat income." And then he does nothing to build the retreat business to reach the $500,000 figure. He somehow got the notion that if he writes a number down on the abstract document called a budget it will happen. Duh… and when it comes December 1, and he is $50,000 away from his projected income number, he panics and tries to make up his deficit with one big swoop called the year-end-letter, appealing to donors for one last big donation to balance his imaginary budget.

Forget your budget!

Concentrate on what it takes to build your business. Concentrate today on what can be done to bring in more retreats and summer campers. Where do you start? Start with the guests who are not coming to your camp. Start by asking direct questions to pastors. "What is keeping you from using our facility?" And then **shut up** and let them tell you without you trying to justify deficiencies and the lack of good service or food. Once you have heard enough details from a variety of groups and churches, go home and dig in.

Dig in and review your menus. Dig in and understand your culture and see how you have created obstacles and ineptness because of rules and systems you have in place. Dig in and understand if there are staff who create an atmosphere of, "Follow our rules, be here when we say, and don't ask for extra program stuff if you didn't write it down five months ago." Look at your facility. Look closely at your facility and your staff.

Honest assessment is a must if you want to grow. It is the little things that add up to a big thing which causes a group to choose another facility to host their retreat.

Our retreat director recently went to Colorado where she and her husband and friends rented a house while the men snowmobiled nearby. Their first night was met with a plugged toilet that was un-flushable and with a bathtub that was backing up too.

105

The owner's first response was, "We can get you into another house tomorrow, but for now, we can't do anything." I asked our retreat director, "How did you feel when you were told that? As the guest, paying the bill, did the thought of four people using a toilet that didn't flush make you feel that your problem was the owner's problem?" I think you know her answer.

Often, camps want to chase new groups with better and brighter marketing. But why spend the money if you don't understand and do something about issues at your camp? A group may try you once, but if you don't live up to your marketing hype, you won't see the group again. Build on repeat business— let other camps have the group who always thinks another camp will provide just one more, better option for them.

I personally study restaurants and hotel facilities to see what makes them tick. I look for what makes me content and happy as a consumer. How was the room presented? What did staff do to make me feel cared for and appreciated? Did I smell any strange odors? Was the food tasty and nutritious and ample? Was the pool clean, warm and available? Did the pictures in the brochure or website match what I am experiencing as a guest? What I feel and perceive as a consumer is exactly how your guests feel and interpret your camp and your camp staff. Don't view them in the abstract; view the interaction as reality. Reality has emotions that create a feeling of value or of being ripped off by price, taste or comfort.

I am a facilities guy. I love to build. I love to see buildings be remodeled. At my camp, we have enough money to do both, and we do both at the same time. Old should be fixed and the new should meet a need. However, if you are struggling to buy a new vacuum or have to think about purchasing 10 gallons of paint, you are in a deep hole. A hole that feels nearly impossible to escape.

I recently visited a very small camp located in the city limits. There were just 10 acres and six buildings. The camp was nearly 50 years old. The new director commented, "When we came, there were piles of junk, discarded furniture, and unused equipment laying around. The only thing we could afford to do was clean up, pick up, and put things away. And after we did that, our guests began to comment how nice things were looking. We did not spend a dime renovating any of our buildings." I knew these people were on the right track of bringing new life back into the camp. Do first things first, even before you create the four-color brochure or update the website: clean and throw away the junk.

Assess, assess, and assess some more! Don't settle as did Micawber; when you get out and hustle, the Lord can provide!

CHAPTER 14

Actions Speak Louder than Words

We should ask of leaders, "What do they stand for? What are their values? Can we trust them?" Not "Do they have charisma?" We've had too much charisma the last hundred years. Truman was the best president the United States has had, and the one who accomplished the most. He was not a high-profile leader— on the contrary, everybody underrated him, including himself. So I have very little use for the superman CEO.

Joseph Maciariello - *A Year with Peter Drucker: 52 Weeks of Coaching for Leadership Effectiveness*

As camp directors, we are on display. Our staff watches us. Our guests watch us. Donors watch us. They in turn react to what they see.

Many of us want to be liked. We want to be popular. We want our charisma and our personality to carry us. We struggle when we have to make tough decisions that will affect the outcome of other people around us. In his book, *9 Things a Leader Must Do*, Henry Cloud writes:

"Successful leaders do not make decisions based on the fear of other people's reactions. Successful leaders decide to do what is right first and deal with the fallout second. Successful leaders are going to tick some people off!"

But as a leader, how do we know what we think is the *right* thing? How do we get to a point where we know it is the "right" thing to do?

Much of the decision making processes of all men depends on perspective. And perspective is the accumulation of past encounters with parents, church, and friends. It is not just one thing that influences our own perspective of what is the right thing.

Let me give you an example. When it comes to building new buildings I am a risk taker. I never have all the money in-hand before I start a new building. Is that the right thing to do? It is for me. For another director, his background and training tells him all bases must be covered financially before the first shovel of dirt is turned. Is he right or is he wrong?

However, not all our decisions are that simple. Some involve people and personalities. Some staff don't produce and have to be let go. Some staff have an attitude that needs adjusting. Some staff need to be prodded and encouraged. What is the right thing? What is a director to do when she knows she must show compassion and kindness, but she also needs to be looking out for the long term vitality of the organization she directs?

Camp is pure fun except for the grumpy, non-compliant people. I would absolutely love all of my job if I didn't have to confront people and redirect their thinking and actions. Dealing with staff can be the most exhausting part of a camp director's job. It wears on you as you try to sleep or rest. It wears on you as you are pursuing hobbies and free time. Dealing with staff plays over and over in your mind when you don't want to be watching it.

As Cloud points out, *"Sometimes you are going to tick people off."* Ouch. Not very Christian sounding to me, but it is true. Not everyone will agree to the direction you are leading the camp. Your decisions about a new building, a new hire, a new summer program, or when necessary, the removal of a staff member can cause people to get their noses out of joint. They become ticked off.

In our culture today, youth's opinions are asked for by their teachers and parents. Young people have much more authority to assert their personal tastes and likes. "I don't have to eat that." "I want to stay up late." "I need to use my phone 24/7." You have heard it all before. At our camp, they have to earn a voice. They may have likes or dislikes that go against the culture of the camp. They may want to be selfish with their time and the amount of attention they are willing to give a guest. The "right" thing is for the director to correct their attitudes and their behavior. And in the process, he might tick them off.

They will get over it, or they will move on.

As the director, I do value other people's opinions about how we should proceed with a program or a hire. I do seek out the staff I feel are competent and have enough understanding of our camp culture to advise me. But at the end of the day, it is the director's job to lead. It is his job to make the call that he deems best for the organization in the long-run.

The long-run is the key. Yes, staff's feelings might be hurt. Yes, their favorite program didn't get the green light for now. Yes, the director just axed their pet project. But it is not the director's job to just look at today only. She must be willing to put off something today so that in five years the camp will be financially healthier or programmatically stronger. As Dave Ramsey says, *"Live like no one else today so you can live like no one else tomorrow."*

Let me give you an example. We had a gap program at our camp for students who had finished high school but were not ready to attend college. We had the program for six years when I decided the camp needed to change directions and go with an apprenticeship program that offered specific training for high school graduates who wanted to go into full-time camping. I heard enormous amounts of complaints and noise. I stayed true to my decision. A few people ended up leaving camp because of my decision; I ticked people off.

Directors who do not stay resolute with their decisions become wishy-washy and easily swayed by staff. There is a time to listen, and there is a time to say, "My decision is final."

CHAPTER 15

Say What You Mean!

The single greatest ministry accelerator is overlooked by many leaders. It is not a great strategy. It is not working harder or doing more. It is not having the right people (although that is important). It is not a charismatic leader (and does not require one). It does not require money.
It is clarity!

Tim Addington

There is nothing I dislike more than indecisive people who never give a straight answer. They act like they are running for a political office and don't want to get fenced in by announcing something with a definitive answer. I want to hear "Yes" or "No" and never "Maybe." Maybe usually means, "I don't have the guts to tell you no to your face, so I will kick the decision down the road hoping you will forget what the question was."

I have made mistakes as the director. Most mistakes develop because I answer too quickly or don't take enough time to research the best answer or take enough time to scrutinize a potential hire. At the same time, staff will tell me that they like how I give them an answer to their question immediately. The staff knows they are free to continue with a program or go and make a decision regarding a retreat group or a purchase. Quick, exact responses to questions increase speed and efficiency of the organization.

It is difficult for new directors to make quick decisions; you simply don't have enough history with the organization to make an off-the-cuff decision. There could be unknown board policies that a decision would violate. There could be a gift-in-kind from a donor that needs to be preserved and not tossed recklessly by a staff member. It could just boil down to not knowing if it is financially feasible. It is acceptable not to know and not to make a snap decision.

It is not okay to start speaking in gobbledygook language that *sounds* like you know what you're talking about, but you are just repeating a bunch of gibberish that sounds official. Statements like, "The board said." Or, "The insurance company won't let us." Or how about my favorite, "It is not in the budget, so I don't think we can do that."

If you are just getting started leading a camp staff you need to prove yourself as their leader. They are looking to you for answers. They want to know where you are heading and how you are going to get there. The quickest way for you to become the leader that the staff will follow is to be clear about your decisions. You need no training or any books on methodology, you simply need a backbone. In his book *Switch, How to Change Things when Change is Hard*, Chip Heath says:

"Ambiguity is the enemy. Any successful change requires a translation of ambiguous goals into concrete behavior. In short, to make a switch, you need to script the critical moves."

Longevity on the job will allow you to answer quicker to questions. New camp directors need to be careful not to answer so quickly that their credibility is diminished by too many wrong decisions. The best way a new director can answer some questions is to flat out say, "I don't know that answer, but if you give me until noon tomorrow I will find out and give you an answer." It wasn't a maybe, and not an, "I will pray about it," it was a clear and concise reply.

Say yes, or no, or give me until tomorrow to find out. Never say maybe.

CHAPTER 16

Maximizing the Staff

Leadership is often misunderstood. When people hear that someone has an impressive title or an assigned leadership position, they assume that individual to be a leader. Sometimes that's true. But titles don't have much value when it comes to leading. True leadership cannot be awarded, appointed, or assigned. It comes only from influence, and that cannot be mandated. It must be earned. The only thing a title can buy is a little time— either to increase your level of influence with others or to undermine it.

John Maxwell - *The 21 Irrefutable Laws of Leadership*

You have the biggest office in the welcome center. You have a name plate on the door. Your office may have the most windows with the best view. You are in charge. You must be a leader. But hold on… there is more to it than that. You have the title. You will need to work at leading.

According to a recent survey by the Ken Blanchard Company:

"47% of new supervisors (directors) receive no supervisor training, and it is usually not received until year 10 – that

gives a person 10 years to flounder on his own. 60% of managers with no training under-perform during their first two years. And first-time managers are shaped by their experiences in the first year, influencing their leadership styles throughout their career."

Consider this book a part of your training. There are some things you must learn, and there are other things you must earn.

As Maxwell states, *you will have to earn it!* You will earn it by doing the right things, at the right time, for the right reason. And as slowly as you can earn your role as a leader of the camp, you can lose it very quickly.

Good decisions and implementation of great ideas move a camp forward. It will increase the retreat load and it will ensure that your summer ministry will be successful. The first year might be considered beginners luck. The second successful year, staff are beginning to line up behind you — they are beginning to trust you. After three years of creating momentum and building the business, the staff will become loyal; you can now make a mistake and they will continue to follow you.

That is why your first two years are critical for your long-term success. You have been reading long-term directors' chapters. Every one of them made some big mistakes in their leadership and decision-making processes. There were more mistakes later in their time of directing the camp, because they were more confident and were willing to experiment and try new programs. They could afford a few mistakes after establishing themselves.

When I began, I was cocky, brash, and opinionated. I pushed things through. I did not surround myself with people to give me advice. I lucked out. Perhaps it was because the camp was brand new and there was no history, no systems, no traditions, and no

"We don't do it that way" from staff or board. And, I only had two staff members under me, and they had even less experience in camping than I had.

If you are taking over the helm at an established camp with existing staff in place, you are walking into a chicken house where all eyes turn to watch your every move. One quick, unsuccessful move on your part will create noise and havoc amongst the chickens; feathers and dust will fly. Eggs will stop being laid due to lack of trust.

Does that mean you do nothing? Absolutely not! Does that mean you have to go around and ask each staff their opinion? Does that mean you need to be extra cautious? It means you better get it right. Do the research. Know exactly the results you want. Know the correct amount of dollars it will cost, and then make sure you complete it at that price. Due diligence means don't screw up.

Being a leader is not about getting a consensus. It is not about allowing everyone to voice an opinion. It is not about a vote by all staff to pick the best option. Being a leader is allowing the process of listening, prodding, and poking at all ideas and then picking the best path. Being the leader is looking ahead and seeing what is on the horizon and making decisions today that will allow the camp to be ready for the future.

Several years ago I could see that people's diets were changing. I was reading about the consumer wanting to know who grew their food and how it was grown. I could see that our menu was not healthy enough for the millennial crowd. I made the decision we were going to shift our menus to a healthier plan. Did I get some resistance? Sure I did. The cook thought I was attacking her when I first suggested the change. Did I go around asking the staff's opinion? No. I had read enough from non-camping publications that showed me a trend ahead. I reacted, and now today, my decision from five years ago has been validated. The millennials are happy!

Had I got it wrong, I would have had to eat crow, go back and admit my stupidity, and let the cooks cook their way. As a new director, you won't have the luxury of taking the risk of making a mistake – you need several right decisions in a row. And remember, crow does not taste good and the feathers will get stuck in your teeth!

CHAPTER 17

Fighting Factions

I once attended a meeting where it seemed that everyone was focused on the people or relationships in a business and believed that doing so would bring success. Don't believe it. Great leaders focus on achieving BOTH task excellence and relationship excellence. This dual focus produces sustainable superior performance. Managers who are solely task focused eventually burn people out. Managers who are solely relationship focused don't set sufficiently high performance standards and challenge the team to accomplish them. However, managers who focus on task and relationship excellence inspire their teams to work together to reach their goal. When the team does reach the goal, the resulting sense of pride inspires, engages and energizes the team to keep performing at the top of their game.

Michael Stallard of Fox Business

Great coaches call great plays and have great players to execute the plays. Poor coaches can call poor plays and have great players fail. Great players can have poor coaches and can execute good plays. It works best when all team members and the coach are working well together and understand how they will win the game.

Camp directors can be great directors, but if the camp staff lacks skills and everyone has different objectives or ideas about how to make the camp successful, there will not be many winning seasons. Success as a director has little to do with how well you know the business or how creative you are with programming. If you can't motivate the staff to work together, your effectiveness will be stifled. Will you be able to run an average camp? Sure. But you will never feel like you are in your groove.

As a matter of fact, not only will you not feel the groove, but you will feel more ruts in the road than you want to deal with on a daily basis. A rutted road is travelable, but not comfortable.

Let me give you an example. I am a frugal camp director. I will pack a sandwich and water when I travel so I don't have to pay $5.99 for a hamburger en route. I will walk around buildings turning off lights. I will work at saving a dollar by getting free shipping or attempt to buy on sale. Am I cheap? No, just extremely careful – with emphasis on the word extreme.

Many years ago, I had a staff member whose answer to me when I asked how much something cost would always be, "It is not much." He lasted less than two years. Was he good at what he was hired to do? I would grade him a B employee. Definitely good enough to continue working for me. However, it was his one attitude regarding buying things that bugged me to no end. I could not get him to see things my way. He had other issues that eventually forced him to leave, but while he worked for me, his lack of frugality and carefulness worked on me. I could not fully trust him with a credit card; I always had to keep my eye on him.

Did I want to? No. I wanted him to fit in so well that any decision he made would be close enough to our corporate way of thinking that a little variance would be acceptable. I wanted him to make enough great decisions that if and when he strayed off course a bit, it was easy to see it as an aberration and not a norm.

Great coaches want to give their team the ability to play on the field without his interference from the bench. Great camp directors want to lead, without constantly second guessing and micromanaging staff. But how is this possible?

Staff need to understand how building trust works; a leader will talk often and long about building trust with him. Staff meetings should be peppered with incidents and examples on how staff can build their trust accounts with the director. When a staff member cooks a great breakfast for 400 with an understaffed kitchen I let her know how much confidence I have in her abilities. When the 20-year-old apprentice steps in and manhandles the dishwasher duties with speed, I let him know how he is building value in himself and how much I trust him.

Steven Covey was right when he wrote in *The Speed of Trust*, "trust adds speed to an organization, and lack of trust makes the price of doing business cost more." When directors trust, there is no time wasted micromanaging. When a director trusts, she doesn't have to be present at the kitchen or the climbing tower to make sure all things go well and things are done her way.

I have been told that I have my ways. You can interpret that to mean, "It is Earl's way, or the highway." I have been told I micromanage people at times. I would not disagree.

Why do I need to micromanage when I see staff not doing things the way I told them? Culture. I have spent years and years developing the culture of camp, and when a new hire comes in and wants to change it, I am going to re-adjust their thinking.

As a new director, with not enough experience, this can be a detriment. You are like the Jr. Senator who is trying to be president.

You know some things well, but perhaps you don't have a clear picture of how all things work together. You get that we need our churches on our team, acting as a cheerleader; but you don't know how church politics vary from church to church and who will decide how and if the camp gets promoted with visits or even if they will allow a brochure display. You know the value of the maintenance man and how necessary he is to the operation, but you do not have enough history of understanding unseen pumps and motors that make all things function properly at camp. You have attended enough fund-raising workshops and seminars that you have a basic understanding of what "should" be done, but you have no networks or donor friends you can call on initially. At this point, you have to fake it until you figure it out.

Faking works for a while. Faking works as long as the rest of the staff doesn't see through your scripted answers that sound similar to a commercial on television. Faking works if you are able to keep enough people in the dark. Fake it until you make it.

Fake it for a season, but there comes a point where you need to produce some results. Results that you personally created. Results that started as your idea and you the director drove it each step of the way. You made outlines of the program or you drew the floor plan to a new building. You created the promotion material and then you raised the money. You raised the money, then you bought the tools and supplies to build. And you supplied the help to get it built. Start to finish – it was your baby.

I have seen where the director has some great big plan that will change everything; usually it is a building. Talk, talk, talk. Maybe he takes it to the second phase where there is an actual drawing by an architect, maybe only a floor plan with a computer CAD program. The entire staff gets all excited about the possibilities, and then nothing happens. I have literally seen camps have projects on the table and with plans that have gone on for 15 years. 15 years is enough time to lose interest. 15 years of planning can give too many people too much time to discuss the project and begin bickering.

There are many things a new director can do to sabotage his directorship. There is one that will absolutely kill it: unfulfilled ideas, plans, and promises.

There is not one of the directors who has written in this book who would not consider themselves dreamers. Each one had to take a blank piece of paper and build something great: a building, a program, a method, or a staff. All current reality started as a wild-haired idea that probably was thought impossible at the time. I personally have done it a hundred times. Big idea, talk, drawing, talk, more talk, re-work the drawing, talk- bam… reality. Footings, floors, walls, roofs, paint, trim, carpet. Bam… the finished product.

How do you put legs onto your ideas? How do you drive a project to done? It is an art. It does take a certain type of personality. It does take a pit-bull mentality that grabs hold and will not release. It does take a pinch of stubbornness, a steady backbone, and resolve. The same focus that a quarterback uses when the game is on the line and he has less than two minutes to drive the length of the field. There is urgency.

John Kotter in *A Sense of Urgency* says this:

> *"The dictionary tells us that urgency means "of pressing importance." When people have a true sense of urgency, they think that action on critical issues is needed now, not eventually, not when it fits easily into a schedule. Now means making real progress every single day. Critically important means challenges that are central to success or*

survival, winning or losing. A sense of urgency is not an attitude that I must have the project team meeting today, but that the meeting must accomplish something important today."

Urgency is used in the kitchen when lunch is 15 minutes away; drop everything and only concentrate on getting the food finished and out to the serving line– dishes can wait and so can supper prep. Urgency is used in the office when summer camp information must be in the mail yesterday; don't worry about retreats or schedules – everyone works at getting the packets stuffed and in the mail– NOW.

Urgency can be confused with a nervous director. A rattled director. An out of control director. Use it sparingly and only if the results that you want really DO need to be finished at a specific time.

CHAPTER 18
My Story - Tom Robertson

Tom Robertson lives out the values he writes about. On a recent tour of Fort Wilderness with other CCCA conference goers, it was evident that every building and every program is tied back to his belief and culture that he has created with personal relationships. His gentle, humble spirit exudes his caring and empathetic heart. www.fortwilderness.com

(Author's Note)

For people to understand me, they have to understand my history. The camp where I am now executive director was started by my parents. In 1956, my parents were looking for a place to start a camp in the north woods. They were brought to our present site, on Spider Lake in McNaughton, Wisconsin. My Dad walked all over the property and made an offer for half of the asking price. The owners accepted the offer and my Dad got it for $8000. Some friends from Indiana came by for a visit on their way to vacation and my Dad gave them a tour. On their way back from vacation, they dropped off a check for $5,000. The value of that gift today is $42,000. That was quite a gift to fund a man's dream!

My Dad was the first executive director of camp and loved the idea of wilderness camping, getting kids out of the city and into God's creation. Dad instinctively understood that God speaks through His creation. Many people ask me how we came up with the name Fort Wilderness. The original founding name was Crusade Camp. Not a very inspiring name, to say the least! Dad was a wordsmith and liked to come up with unique names, so he used a Thesaurus extensively. One day he was looking up cowboy words and stumbled across the word "fort" (a place of refuge). Since he loved creation and the wilderness, it was pretty easy to put the two together. Fort Wilderness was born. A fort was a stronghold, good word! Dad was a pastor, so Christian was important to include. Adventure was important also, so that was the beginning of our tagline, "Stronghold of Christian Adventure."

Dad wanted us to have a western influence so horses became a large part of our programming; his idea was to give campers experiences that they could not have at home so consequently, we were not big into traditional sports. We have not been a sports-oriented camp to this day.

From the beginning, horses were a big part of camp. Our first horse was old Joe, a swaybacked old horse, soon followed by Dickey, Pride, Lucky and Buck and hundreds more. Outdoor cooking and fire building, archery, riflery, swimming, canoeing, camp-outs, and hiking were the major programs. Early morning exercise and the morning dip before breakfast were mandatory – it was the only way to have campers smell clean throughout the week! Morning chapel was also highly important. During high school camp, we had chapel twice a day. It was morning and evening with a guest speaker. Camp in the early days was two weeks long and all the cabins had triple high bunk beds.

I am the third of five kids born to Truman and Janice Robertson. According to birth order study, a middle child tends to be a people pleaser, thrives in friendships, has a large social circle and is a peacemaker. I can see parts of each of these characteristics in who I am. I think they also play to my strengths today. In the early days of camp, we kids were given more responsibilities than we would allow kids to have today. I started to drive when I was 13, started outdoor cooking for campers at 14, led horseback rides and worked in the barn.

When I was a sophomore, I was the ski instructor and boat driver every summer until I graduated from college. I was popular with the girls– just imagine…sun bleached hair, bronzed body, cut-off jeans as a swim suit and believe it or not, I was in great shape from all that skiing and swimming. I said imagine!!!

My brothers Ron, Paul and Steven and sister, Nancy were all involved in areas of programming. Being given lots of responsibility early defined all five of us children. We are all leaders in our spheres of influence. Our parents instilled in us a high value in relationships and taught us by example. So I have a natural aptitude for the position I have held for 20 years as executive director. I can't help it, I enjoy people.

Like my Dad, I have also had a vision for Fort Wilderness. I wanted Fort to be a place where campers could come and hear about Jesus and the importance of having Him be the Savior of life. I wanted campers to encounter and live out a personal relationship with the Creator of the universe Who died on the cross for our sins.

I also wanted to have Fort be a safe place for campers to come and have adventures. Those adventures are different for different groups. Family campers need time to just be with their families doing the many varied activities, and yet taking time to slow down from the hectic pace of life and be a family again. They eat meals together, swim or canoe together, go to the woodshop, craft shop or the nature center. Maybe more importantly, they all sleep together in the same tent, cabin or RV.

For youth campers, their adventure is to go on a camping trip and sleep in a tent for the first time or swim in a real lake, fish, throw a tomahawk or ride a horse. We want them to be immersed in God's creation, to see the Milky Way at night or sit around a campfire with their cabin mates while their counselor tells them about Jesus' love for them. Camp needs to be that place where it's safe for you to talk about struggles where no one will condemn you or put you down. Instead, the people here will walk with you through the hurt and give you hope in The One Who loves you with an everlasting love.

After college, I returned to camp and continued to be a part of the leadership team. My wife Jean and I had married in 1972 after graduating from Grand Rapids School of the Bible and Music. Jean grew up as a missionary kid in rural Nebraska. Her Dad, as part of his responsibility, ran a small summer only Bible camp.

Jean said she never wanted to do three things: cook for large groups, work in an office or live in a mobile home. *Never tell God what you don't want to do because you end up doing them.* That's exactly what Jean did at Fort Wilderness in those early years, all three of them!

We have three grown daughters, three fine sons-in-law and four grandkids. My wife and I both worked at camp until we had kids, working, building, cleaning and leading groups in activities. I eventually became the director of operations.

In 1986, my Dad got a blood clot in his right lower leg and after a month, he had to have it amputated. And in 1988, he retired from the executive director position. There had been no discussion for a succession plan up to this point. We were in a leadership crisis and the board, doing what good boards do, went out to find a director. Dad was not good at money matters so the board went out to find a strong financial person. This scenario played itself out over the next seven years.

In the rush to find leadership, one of the most important ingredients that made Fort Wilderness, The Fort, was missing. That ingredient was *culture*. The driving culture was caring about people but it was not considered in the search for leadership. The other issue is that the board and staff never clearly defined our values. I will discuss these issues later on.

So because these two questions, "Who are we?" and "What drives us?" were not answered, there was disconnect in choosing the next leaders. The two directors hired between 1987 and 1992 were great guys, but they didn't get who we were. There was no alignment.

For seven years Fort struggled with leadership, of which I was a part. I got to the place where I was done with the struggle. I had held onto Fort as an owner. Dad started the camp so in a way, I felt it was mine. It was totally illegitimate ownership. I finally had had enough and gave camp up to the Lord. "God, Fort has never been mine, it's Your camp, and I don't want it. If You want me here, OK, but I am done." I was free for God to use me however He wanted.

The following year, through a lot of circumstances, I was named the new executive director of Fort Wilderness. It was December of 1995. As my friend, Ed McDowell of Warm Beach Camp and

Conference Center, Stanwood, Washington shared, I needed to settle the glory issue. Either I got it or God got it. I was not meant to carry the glory belonging to God. It was so freeing to lay that burden down.

Since the beginning of my tenure as director, our camp has grown considerably. We have grown from a camp with a $750,000 budget with 10 staff in 1995 to a $3.2 million dollar budget with 20 staff and 8 interns in 2015.

We were primarily a kids' camp when we began, now we have 3 areas of camp to encompass different types of groups all seasons of the year:

Main Camp – In the summer, Main Camp runs one junior high camp and 8 weeks of family camp. We have various fall and winter camps as well. A new addition to Main Camp is a large building called the Eagles' Roost, which houses 10 young adults in an eight month discipleship program called TruNorth.

Adventure Outpost – This camp is primarily for third through eighth grade kids in the summer.

Leadership Lab – This camp runs a summer program for high school kids. It is a three week program that runs three times a summer and includes outdoor adventure and Bible teaching to allow kids to explore their faith and make it their own.

VALUES

As I alluded to earlier, the values by which we live and develop Fort are the power of God's Word, the majesty of creation, developing deep, long-lasting relationships and adventure programming. These are the driving forces that propel Fort today and are weaved through everything we do. With the four original values as a guide, we have moved our camp forward to meet the needs of the culture of today.

The Word of God. Fort Wilderness is a place where campers come to hear about Jesus and the importance of having Him be the Savior of life. I want campers to know they can have a personal relationship with the Creator of the universe Who died on the cross for our sins. We nurture an environment to make that happen.

When our campers come to Fort Wilderness, their world is shifted. They are sleeping in a different bed, the food is different, their schedule is different, and people are different. Their brains are trying to make sense of it, so it opens up the mind to these new experiences. And that's when the Holy Spirit begins to work because their minds are open to new teachings. This is the power and genius of the temporary camp community.

We place a high value on the *cleanliness of our camp, the comfort of our cabins and the quality of our food.* If the campers are not thinking about just having had the worst meal ever, or the bad sleep they had last night or that the cabins were filthy… We want to sweep away all those objections. Then they are going to hear the Gospel and they are going to hear the things that are presented to challenge them to live their lives a different way.

And *the Gospel has to be shared in its entirety.* Not just that we are sinners and that Christ died for us. We need to talk about God creating this perfect world, Adam and Eve and their free will to obey Him or not. If you do not understand where sin came from, sin doesn't make any sense to this culture. The kids do not get it. What are you talking about? They just say, "I'm not a sinner." If we talk about Adam and Eve's disobedience and that sin came into the world, we have context for them to understand that we have sin now. God's remedy was to send the perfect Sacrifice.

But that is not the end of it either. The purpose is that we are going to reunite with God the Father at the end of time. So, it just becomes a whole story that we get to tell, not just the middle. In this culture, when we tell the whole story, it's a different story. And then, they are able to relate to it.

Every camp may have a different approach to sharing the Gospel. What needs to be considered is what drives each camp to choose the philosophy they have adopted. *Everyone in camp ministry says that our purpose is the Gospel. How the Gospel is delivered is the philosophy of each camp.*

Then, the philosophy of how the Gospel is delivered needs to reach through all decisions. One place in particular that a camp needs to focus on is choosing specific programs or events.

For example, many have rope courses. We need to ask, what is the purpose of the ropes course? Is the ropes course about understanding who you are as a person? There's nothing wrong with that, but what is the greater purpose? Not JUST that you get a sense of accomplishment, which is important for some kids, but that *sense of accomplishment does <u>what</u> for the Kingdom of God?* We have to think that through.

Campers are going to come to camp, learn some cool stuff, do some cool things, but it is not all about the experience. Part of it is the experience and part of it is what you're going to learn through the experience. *However, we also want to build into their lives.*

Majesty of Creation. I want Fort Wilderness to be a place where campers can be immersed in God's creation. We can know God through His creation. *We do not worship the creation, we* *worship the Creator.* We are very careful at directing our curriculum towards God's creation.

We have a Nature Center at Main Camp. The Nature Center teaches classes that focus on God's creation. When we started the Nature Center, I wanted Michael Lane, the Nature Center director to take God's creation and use it to allow campers to be able to study and to learn spiritual truth. God says we can know Him by His creation.

The Heavens declare the glory of God; the skies proclaim the work of his hands. Day after day they pour forth speech; night after night they display knowledge. There is no speech or language where their voice is not heard. Their voice goes out into all the earth, their words to the ends of the world. Psalm 19:1-4

Another area where we intentionally give campers the ability to spend time in God's creation is at the men's and women's retreats. We let campers come in a day early and encourage them to have silence and solitude for most of the day on Friday. It was a decision to create an opportunity for them to slow down and hear the still small voice of the Creator, as Scripture tells us. We are so busy in our lives, *there's so much noise in our lives that we don't give people time to slow down and begin to contemplate scripture, outdoors in God's creation where God speaks to us.*

Deep, Long-Lasting Relationship. Camp, to me, needs to be that place where it is safe for you to talk about struggles, where no one will condemn you. Instead, we will walk with you through the hurt and give you hope in The One Who loves you with an everlasting love.

That's why it has to be about the people! An important adage to remember is, *"the most important person is the person in front of you."* We get caught up in doing the stuff, but we have to decide...why are we doing this? *Camp is about people.*

When you think about carrying your values through the organization, you even have to think about how you're going to build your buildings and run your programs based on your values.

Relationships are so important to Fort Wilderness that when we build or remodel buildings, our staff talk about *where we create space for people to build relationships.* We added booths to our Gathering Place, where all the chapel services are held and people meet to visit between services. We built a coffee shop called Camp Grounds, knowing it was a place for people to hang out. It was an intentional decision. All the cabins have a table and benches to create community and relationships in each cabin. When the Adirondack chairs are built to set in areas around camp, there's a purpose behind that. It reinforces the value of relationship.

Another example of weaving our values into every decision is when we designed the septic system for 300 beds at Main Camp. When we did this, our capacity went from 200 to 300 campers. We were starting to grow and we could have made the septic system larger. My philosophy was that the bigger your camp gets, the less personal it gets. So you have to make a choice, how big do you want to get? *Is big the only indicator of success?* The higher quality and better experience you can provide is just as much a part of camp growth as how big you get. It does not have to be numerical to be successful. *The value of relationship guided my path.*

Our full-time staff is here because we want to connect with people. We are the ones who are taking hikes and having campfires and interacting with the people. We want the campers to feel that they are a part of what is going on at camp. We are not a rental camp, which would not value the relationship between staff and campers as much as we do.

Adventure Programming: I want Fort Wilderness to be a safe place for campers to come and have an adventure. How do we give campers a camp adventure? *Be aware of an atmosphere that you can develop to foster adventure. Do things that are new and different.*

Here are some things that can open your mind to creating an atmosphere.

At Leadership Lab, it's a tradition to read *Tales of the Kingdom* around the campfire. Every kid loves an adventure book. The staff tell stories around the campfire, we can embellish them a little bit. Your memory changes over time, you know.

My wife Jean still remembers a night in the summer of 1971 at high school camp. All the kids were awakened up at midnight for a pancake feast in the dining hall. The counselors had hung a tin can light from the ceiling and after breakfast, we had singers and guitar players sing songs from that decade. Jean can still see and hear them, feel the atmosphere from that night, almost 45 years ago!

We always look for ways to delight campers, get people to laugh. My brother Ron has a happy-go-lucky spirit and has done the announcements for family camp for many years. He delights us all of the time because of his sense of humor. One time he told us that we were going to have a Kirby salesman come and do a demonstration class for family campers, because a long time ago, he bought a Kirby vacuum with a new attachment. The attachment was a table saw and that is how he built a 4-bedroom house!

We have to have a sense of humor, and we have to be able to laugh at ourselves; we have a tendency to take ourselves too seriously. And we don't need to take offense if campers remember something goofy we did.

Our philosophy to do things that are new and different is why we don't have a gym. The campers would come to camp and go to the gym because that is what they do at home. We do not want them to do that. We want them to have new experiences. We want them to be out on the lake, on a stand-up paddle board, canoeing and kayaking. We want them to go up to Black River Harbor in Michigan and jump into the waterfalls. Those are things that they can't do at home.

At kid's camp, we have a philosophy about competition. I don't think competition is bad, you want to teach kids how to win, but it is not all about winning. It is about playing the game. There is a certain value in just playing, no over-coaching of kids. Just enjoy the experience. A game is a game. It can just be fun.

We have a game at night called a snipe hunt at Adventure Outpost. A snipe hunt is about the lore, about something new. Nobody wins and nobody loses, it's just a game. The kids are told by their counselors to get their pillow cases to catch snipe, so they go out in the woods for 2 hours with bags trying to catch snipes. The kids don't know that snipes aren't real, it's about the adventure.

We always drive the idea that camp is fun, even mischievous at times. Camp is a fun place to be. But we also need to be reminded that camp ministry is not just to create opportunities for people to have recreation. *Recreation is only a tool to be used for a greater purpose, the greater purpose being that we portray Jesus Christ and we share the Gospel.*

LEADERSHIP STRATEGIES

Since those first years of defining our organization, I have found some leadership strategies to be particularly successful. The following is the summation of those strategies.

Stewardship Model of Management: I have tried to manage camp with a stewardship model. Camp is not about me, but it is so easy to have that false sense of ownership. When you get to make all the decisions, then it does become about you. I needed to get "me, mine, my," vocabulary under the lordship of The One Who truly owns the Fort.

I rebel against saying, "my camp," "my staff," or "my board." When I talk about camp I say "our staff" because we are a team, we are all involved together. I say "our board." It is not my board, the board does not belong to me. I work under the leadership of the board. It is the board of Fort Wilderness, we are ministering together.

When you begin to use the personal pronoun I, then it becomes personal, "this is my camp." The reality is, it is not yours. You get to be a steward of the ministry to which God has led you. God gets the glory!

The one thing that helped me grow and be successful as a leader was to *get me out of the way!*

Board: When my Dad was executive director, all the board members were his friends. He had to have a board because of our non-profit status, but my Dad ran the board. He did whatever he wanted to do. He didn't look to the board to help him manage camp, so he created a lot of conflict for himself.

When I became executive director, I told the board that I expected them to hold me accountable, help make decisions. They

139

had entrusted me to run camp, I was going to do that. And so, I didn't want them to direct our staff, which was not their job. Their job was to bring leadership to me and oversight to the whole organization. I began to look for board members with aptitude, skill, characteristics and experience that could bring value to the board. I didn't look for members I could control, I wanted members that would challenge me.

One time, I was listening to a speaker on board development who helped me clarify my thinking. He said, "As a director, think about bringing on board members like you would when building a church. If you build a new sanctuary for 30 million, you won't hire a company that has 10 million dollars' worth of experience. You are going to hire a company that has 100 million dollar worth of experience because that company has all the connections and relationships that can be leveraged to help them do a 30 million dollar project with excellence."

So, *if you have a camp budget of 1 million dollars, look for board members who have experience with 10 million dollars.*

I ask our board members not to sit on their experience when we meet. I want their experience to help us take Fort Wilderness down the path to a better version of ourselves. We have board members who work in publishing, personnel, the non-profit sector and finance. Our camp has grown exponentially because we don't have members who are saying, "What did we do last quarter?" We're saying, "How do we go farther and how are we going to leverage camp to meet the needs that are out there?" That is the real value that the board has brought.

I have encouraged the board to come to camp and volunteer so they have a better idea of how camp operates. *Our board is an organizational board.* I do not want the board to direct our staff, but to talk to staff. I want them to ask them how they are doing or for what prayer needs they have. I want the staff and the board to have a sense that we're all in this together. I want the board and the staff to be connected. It is another opportunity for relationship.

Character Attribute: The character attribute that served me best as a camp director would be similar to the "Skipper" from Gilligan's Island. I like people, I like connecting with people, the whole relational part. I'm not condemning. I'm pretty gracious, I think. I like to draw people out, I like for them to tell their story.

My favorite time of day is when our chapel services are done in the late morning. The Gathering Place is an inviting room where all our chapel services are held. I like the time after chapel, sitting in the Gathering Place and continuing what we learned in chapel or just chatting. It's informal, not rushed.

I love the challenge of meeting new people and winning them over. I derive satisfaction from breaking the ice and making a connection. *The skill of building relationship has affected the most success for me as the director. And camp reflects that.*

Staff: My leadership style is inclusive. I am not a dictator. If I have an idea, I ask others what they think about that idea. It is collaborative. No idea is a bad idea. The input of everybody creates something unique. Then the fun factor goes through the roof.

And *camp is not about me, I don't have to be up front. I choose not to be up front.* If it were about me, I would have to be the spokesperson all the time. Everything would have to revolve around my gifts and abilities. I want other staff to shine. I invite them to express who they are and give them opportunity to share their stories. It helps them in their leadership. It helps them get connected to campers in a deeper way. It's important.

But also as a leader, I have specific ideas that are non-negotiable. For example, in the dining hall there is a water pump that has been there since camp started. There was talk about removing it. The water pump is part of who we are and what campers expect, so I said that we are not going to get rid of it. I am going to drive those things for which I have a passion. Because *I believe there have to be traditions that are important, it's part of our corporate story, there are things that people expect and I need to preserve those.*

We have to create opportunities for our staff to connect with people. There's ALWAYS going to be something to do. We are never going to finish a day's work. The next day has another pile of work to be done. Knowing that, work hard, then if we're walking across camp and we see someone who needs to talk, we take 10 minutes and sit down and talk to them. That is the ministry we are in.

We are all, all our staff, we are ministers. We can't minister to people if we can't take time to get to know people.

There are many lessons I've learned in the last 20 years. These are some lessons that I think might be applied universally to camp ministry.

LESSONS I'VE LEARNED

After I became executive director in 1995, I would sometimes let that little voice that chatters in the back of my mind say, "Do you really have what it takes or are you the director because you are Truman's, (my Dad), son?"

I would discount myself and let Satan's accusations some-times hinder the work I was doing. And yet, I knew in God's sovereignty, there was a reason I was made director and I could live in that reality.

Don't discount what God wants to do in your life. If God has directed you into a position of leadership, step into it! Go for it. You will make mistakes, just like I did and still do, but it is through the struggle that we grow and develop as leaders.

Life is never ideal. My Dad used to say this, meaning we will have adversity, we were never promised an easy time of it. It gives us backbone and wisdom in the journey of life. Dad also told us when those hard times come, *"Roll with the punch."* Learn to take a hit but don't let it take you out of the game.

When I was a new camp director, I needed to know who I was. I needed to understand what my strengths and weaknesses were and how my leadership affected the organization I led. Through this experience, I've been able to tell others when looking for a camp in which you will work, consider these things:

- *Understand who you are and what drives you as a person.*
- *Know the values of the organization that you are considering.*
- *If they don't match, don't go there.*
- *If you go to a camp and they can't articulate their values, be cautious about going there.*

I understood the ministry side of camp ministry, but not the business side. Camp requires both ministry and business. It's a two-edged sword. If you don't take care of the business, there will not be a ministry of which to take care. And if you are not taking care of ministry, you are not accomplishing the goal for which you started camp in the first place. I had to learn the business.

One of the ways I've found to be successful in understanding business is to stay in tune with the business world.

Leaders have to be readers. Exercise your leadership brain. Attend conferences to learn from other people. Spend time with men and women who have been successful in business. Focus on what is happening in the culture at large to stay relevant. These have all become habits of mine over the years to allow me to expand my knowledge of business.

This is my journey and my story. When it is all said and done, how have I done with the opportunity to love our campers? *I look at how many times the Apostle Paul challenged us to LOVE. It was over and over.* Gal 5:6 says in paraphrase that faith is expressed through love. So as I finish out my time in Christian camping, I will continue living out the goals of loving people and helping to develop their relationship with the Lord. So my challenge to the reader is...

GO. Write Your Story, and Love People!!

CHAPTER 19
Strategic Planning

A woodpecker could adopt either of two strategies: Peck once on a thousand trees or peck one tree a thousand times. How might you apply this disciplined thinking in your work? What could yield to stubborn persistence?

Glenn Brooke- *A Leader Thinks Aloud*

Much of strategic planning is about what you CAN do now and not what you COULD do in the future.

Strategic planning is just doing things. Some directors love the meeting where ideas are discussed by a group of staff; other directors like to just be doing things... there is strategy in their minds, but it is not written down– it is in their heart and head. Some need dates and plans and strategy laid out on paper; it is a comfort blanket, their road map. Others only need a general idea of what could happen, and are willing to make up the pieces as the years go by. Like Jim Collins says in *Great by Choice*, "They know the beginning and they know the end, and the middle they make up as they go. They don't sweat the middle."

It is really hard to project out five years as to what a camp could be. There are generalities that help make assumptions: if a building is built, retreat revenue will increase; if a program area is developed, summer campers and retreaters are more satisfied and want to return to camp for something new.

Don't hyper-focus on insignificant details and not see the big picture; big picture thinking is more valuable for leaders, but we usually get drug down into figuring menu problems, tractor breakdowns, and details others should be covering and working through.

I have tried bringing the camp board into the strategic planning of the camp. I have tried to get them to see out three or five years. What I have found is that they can't see that far. There is usually only one or two who have that kind of mind, while the rest are quite content talking about all the things we have done or are currently doing well right now.

Initially, pick your strategic planners carefully. Include those around you who are constantly saying, "You know what would be neat to have at camp? Have you ever thought about horses, or cabled bridges, or a lodge built just for high schoolers?" Call them dreamers. Not all men are dreamers; some never sit still long enough to dream. I have not been able to find too many around me who want to dream too large or think out too far. Actually, in today's fast-moving, ever-changing culture I can't think out five years accurately.

"What about a master plan?" you ask. I would say, "Good to have, good to look at once in a while, but don't follow it like it is the Holy Grail. It is a document that well-intentioned people put together at some point in the camp's history that showed some possibilities of the future camp. Some of it was good, some of it was pure imagination." What is important is what can be paid for by donors and completed by the staff.

Strategic planning must be fluid, it must be able to adapt to the changes our world is throwing at us, and it must be able to react to opportunities given to us.

Strategic planning is finding a target and taking aim and hitting a target. Long-range planning is just dreaming. Strategic thinking is doing things that matter.

If you are new to camping, the idea of strategic thinking or strategic planning should be a very vague and abstract idea; it sounds like something you should be doing, but it just is not happening with all the clamor for your time, there are too many things to figure out first.

Initially, spend your energy getting things done right. You will not have enough understanding if they are the right things to be doing to prepare for the future. You will hear from many who are using your camp, "Why don't you build a gym? Why not build a pool? We need a zip line. We want better beds." Their wish and want list usually makes some sense. You know you need to do something, but what needs to happen first?

Let me give you a plan that could work in helping you decide what to do first. It doesn't sound flashy. It is just plain, simple, non-common-core math.

A director needs to assess what needs to be done first. What efforts made today will pay the most dividends tomorrow? With strategic planning, it boils down to results that matter. All other activities and building are important, but those things done now that get results, produce needed income, and provide momentum are the most valuable for growth.

I would tell a director of an older camp that is struggling to pay their bills to focus on their beds and plates. What is keeping people from wanting to eat your food and sleep in your beds? The strategy in these questions is that you are not discussing marketing, church usage, pastors, or youth leaders. It is not discussing lack of donations, or questioning your website's performance. It is only focusing in on *why guests don't want to sleep and eat with you.* You eliminate the hyperbole chatter of "I think" or "I believe" – you will be able to say, "I know."

How can you get answers to this question? Get in your car and travel to talk to former guest group leaders. Get on the phone and make as many contacts with former guest groups as you can. Approach them with a humble spirit, and with an attitude and disposition that is non-threatening. Admit there are deficiencies with your camp and come across as one who wants to hear directly from those making retreat decisions within churches or organizations. Vague questions get vague answers. Be direct.

1. What did we not provide at your last retreat that would have created a better atmosphere for you?
2. What facilities would you like for us to provide? What are we lacking that is important to your group?
3. Did you feel cared for by our staff? Did our staff meet your needs? If not, is that one of the reasons you have not returned?
4. Were there promises made that we did not keep?

Don't stop asking until you begin to see a pattern. Begin to put the puzzle pieces together that will allow you to return home and create an actual strategy to remedy your situation and to provide you with the needed business. Your concentrated focus in this one area has potential to provide the needed cash to continue. If you don't fix this problem, you won't be in existence in five years. There will be no reason to have a five year plan.

Quite frankly, many camps are in denial about their physical condition, their culture and their amenities. Many staff members are living in a cloud of what it was like 15 years ago – they cannot see the world has marched on past them and has higher expectations for facilities, programs and customer service.

Once I found out the reasons, I would attack the problem. Your research HAS told you <u>why</u> you have a lack of funds, lack of usage, lack of momentum: people are not using you for a reason. Fix those things that are keeping people away from using your camp.

For those camps who are moving along, paying the bills, and appear to be doing just okay, but still have too many open weekends, you too have strategic issues to deal with that might be larger than beds and plates. You might be suffering from too many rules or regulations that hamper a retreat group from "feeling at home" while they are with you. There may be a lack of staff engagement with a retreat group. I have heard more than once from a retreat group, "We arrived. Checked in at the office. Went to our lodge and never saw a staff person the entire weekend, unless at meal time – and even then it was the cooks and dishwashers." There was no love and care by the staff.

For the larger camps that seem to have all things going well, you will need to return to some type of master plan; you will need to try to see what you want to be in five years. You will look for new opportunities to minister – whether it is adding completely different programs or even buying another camp at another location. You have your business model in place and will be capable of spending time dreaming of what could be in the future. You can't sit still; it doesn't take long for a camp to begin "the decline."

So my advice: stop spending too much time dreaming about your five year plan. Do something that really matters today, so that in five years, you will have a more sustainable camp. We all want growth so that we can achieve a level of business that will provide enough cash flow to allow the ministry of the camp to be able to accomplish the original mission of the camp: "to see that every boy and girl comes to know Christ."

CHAPTER 20

Know That Not All Hires Will Work Out

*"You can't spend too much time or effort on 'hiring smart'.
The alternative is to manage tough, which is much more
time consuming."*

Gary Rogers, (Chairman & CEO of Dreyers Grand Ice Cream)
from *Hiring Smart* by Dr. Pierre Mornell

We want every hire to fit. We want all new staff to fit in to our culture and add value to our existing systems. And yet, not all people work out. Some walk away disappointed and discouraged about the camping ministry, while others must be released to go work for someone else. Seldom are all parties happy about the separation process.

I have made some great hires. I have made some horrible hires. And so will you. I did nothing different in the process of hiring great people than I did with poor hires. Typically, I do the interview, call some references, and then go with my gut.

According to Dr. Pierre Mornell, in his book, *Hiring Smart*:

"If you make a mistake in hiring, and you recognize and rectify the mistake within six months, the cost of replacing that employee is two and one-half times the person's annual salary."

Unless your camp is different than mine, you can't afford that kind of financial drain on your already meager budget. The wrong hire will be a constant headache whom you must micromanage and in the end, will cause you to shell out even more hard-earned cash in getting rid of and rehiring the right replacement.

Slow down. You can live one more week without a program director or a maintenance man. It will be an inconvenience, but the stakes are too high if you rush in and hire the first available, breathing person to fill a position.

What will make a good staff person at your camp? Skills, personality, attitude, or if she will work cheap and is available right now?

Many times we hire someone who comes highly recommended to us by a friend or a board member of the camp. The new hire has a relationship with someone we trust. Other times, we hire someone because we have heard they can fix anything. I have hired people because I just simply like them. Or, I hire because I get a reference that he is a real worker.

I like how Jon Acuff in his book, *Do Over: Rescue Monday, Reinvent Your Work, and Never Get Stuck*, breaks down why people don't do well in certain jobs, and gives perfect examples of people who have three of the four qualities we are looking for in a person:

- *Relationships + Skills + Character – Hustle = Wasted Potential, NFL Draft Busts, One-Hit-Wonder Bands*

- *Skills + Character + Hustle – Relationships = The Career Version of the Emperor's New Clothes*
- *Character + Hustle + Relationships – Skills = Me in the NBA or Michael Jordan in Baseball*
- *Relationships + Hustle + Skills – Character = Tiger Woods, Enron, Guns N' Roses*

Christian camping has a reputation of hiring from outside the industry. We hire the local youth pastor to become the program director because he is a fun guy and can lead a youth group. We hire an energetic coach to market our camp. We hire a business man who is good with finances to be our office manager.

Here are some of my latest hires. I hired a neighbor 10 years ago to do our books because she worked at a bank and she lived two miles down the road. I hired a retreat coordinator because a board member said she was his niece and was a smart person who had worked at Eli Lilly, but now was working on a dude ranch in Colorado. I hired a program director because he was in need of a job and he had worked on staff many summers ago. I lucked out; they have all been great hires.

I have made as many bad hires as well. I will spare you their positions or what transpired after the hire. They created havoc, distrust, destroyed staff morale, and left very angry at me. They all left believing I knew nothing about running a camp. Ouch.

You create a job description and you go looking for someone to fit the job description to a T. Good luck. If you do find the person who fits perfectly, someone is either lying or they have a too high opinion of themselves. I have studied enough camp job descriptions that unless someone comes with a big S printed on their chest, it won't be a perfect fit.

What can you expect? You can expect that your new hire will not be as talented as he claimed he was in certain areas. You can expect that you will be surprised that a new hire will have outstanding capabilities not even talked about while discussing what the job entailed. You will discover some will lack drive. You will discover some will have too much drive and end up alienating other staff with their bossiness and opinions. You never will get exactly what you thought you were getting.

So now what do you do? Fire the person because she is not an exact fit? Heavens, no! You adjust your expectations. You pull responsibilities that this hire has no talent or interest in and give those responsibility to someone else. You add projects and responsibilities where there are strengths.

I hired a young lady several years ago. I wanted her to take over the duties of the retreat coordinator who was retiring. In our interview, we discussed the possibilities of marketing to new groups. She nodded and said, "I could do that," and I assumed since she was pleasant, outgoing, and personable, that she could and would do some marketing. What I found out after six months without a trip away from camp by this new hire was that she was a bit reserved and even a bit "nerdy," and liked creating staff assignment sheets and putting together the managing details for a weekend retreat. She was great at assigning staff to responsibilities and charting it out on an hour by hour spread sheet, which told everyone where to be at what time and what they were to do. Once I saw that ability, there was no more talk about church visits and marketing; I had stumbled onto a hidden gift that was ten times more valuable to me. We hired someone else whose whole life was about marketing.

I do wish I could **Do Over** on my hires. If I could, here is what I would do:

- I would move slower.
- I would not trust the references given to me by the applicant. I would try to find references further down the line from those listed on the application. I would dig deeper.
- I would look at character, hustle, skill, and their ability to work as a team member.

Jon Acuff is correct. It does take all four elements to make a great employee. Is there any one trait that trumps the others? I don't think so. If one trait is out of whack, it can skew the entire performance.

However, if there was one element I could accept as the weakest, it would be skill. I can teach skill. I can teach someone to enter computer data. I can teach someone to cook. I can teach someone to clean or paint or build. I can't teach character and hustle. I can't teach someone to be teachable. I can't teach someone to not be territorial. I can't teach someone to look after the interest of others, before themselves.

We hired an intern 10 years ago. Straight A student throughout college. Nice young lady who had accepted Christ at our camp when she was 10 years old. She had majored in history in college without a teacher certification; there are not many jobs out there for history majors. She came to work for $200 per week as a housekeeper and kitchen helper. No prior skills in either area, however, she had worked for us during college years in the summer.

She learned to cook. She learned to clean. She cleaned thoroughly and with precision. We moved her up to assistant cook. She learned more skills. She became a lead cook on a shift. She did less housekeeping. We paid her more. We needed help in the office with computers and data entry. She accepted the challenge and proved herself worthy. We increased her load in the office and eliminated housekeeping. She kept learning new skills. Today she is completely out of the kitchen and housekeeping because of a new-found and developed skills set and now works as our coordinator for our programmed retreats.

And during the entire process of several years, she showed she had the right attitude. She was teachable. She worked with diligence and integrity. She finished her jobs to the exact detail. She was a team player and would go out of her way to help other staff. She accepted her role as an assistant to others and did not overstep her authority.

And I have experienced just the opposite.

I have hired people who have had all the skills. But they came in with an attitude. They came in and thought they understood more than they actually knew about working in a camp. They would not work together with other staff. They had the actual skills to run programs or be a builder or the maintenance man, but they couldn't work together with others. Some could not be trusted to finish their job. Others lacked integrity.

I share my perspective to show that sometimes you will get burned. Sometimes you will be pleasantly surprised. How can you know when you have a winner after reading a resume, having an interview, and contacting references? One way to find out what the new hire is made of is to offer him a position that is below the person's perceived skill set. Hire him into a lesser position without authority over anyone else first. Hire a person and let him grow into a bigger position. It is much easier to move someone up quickly than to try to move them back down the ladder. I will never hire someone into a senior management position, unless I am able to watch him work further down the chain of command. Use the word assistant before you use the word director.

I know you are saying, "I need a head cook now. It is May and summer is coming!" We have all been there. You take a chance. You listen to the references, go with your gut and hope and pray for it to work out well. It will work out sometimes, it won't other times. There are times for expediency and there are times for caution. And, there is a difference between a summer position and a full-time position; I know I can endure anyone for eight weeks – I cannot endure everyone for an extended time.

In order to make a great hire, you must know what your camp culture looks like, acts like, and how it delivers services to guests. If the camp is a loosey-goosey camp that has few rules and runs by the seat of its pants weekend after weekend, an OCD-type of person would not fit. If you, as an analytical director, need plans, details, budgets, and cost all completed in triplet form prior to the first board being purchased for a cabin, you don't want to hire a ram, cram, slam type of builder that to whom speed is everything.

Not all staff will fit in well with the director's culture.

There are all types of camp cultures. I have seen quiet, reserved camps. I have seen wild and crazy and adventurous camps. I have seen peaceful and timid camps. I have seen innovative, risk-taking camps. I have seen camps full of rules and regulations. The director's personality can make up the operational culture into which a new hire must fit well.

If you, as the director, have a certain bent about your attitudes, behavior, and likes, you will affect the culture. As a matter of fact, much of what the director believes important will become the camp culture. As the director, you are able to manage and develop cultural aspects of the camp. You do this by education, by adjusting the budget to match your desires, and you just sometimes lay out policy and procedure that dictates "this is the way we will do things." You, as the director, should know the culture and live it consistently.

I am big on hustle. I like seeing staff move quickly and efficiently. If the maintenance man takes a trip to the shop, he had better not have a truckload of staff in the front seat of the truck to pick up one tool. I don't like dinkers. I don't want staff standing around talking about what they just did in detail. I want work to be done on the run. So, why would I hire someone who, in an interview, talks about building deep, intimate relationships? I want production and she wants relationships. It will be like two bulls in the same pasture.

As the director, you had better understand yourself enough to know what you find as acceptable behavior and work habits. It is true we like to be around people who are like-minded. I am a Republican: I like to be around people who are Republicans. I do not like to be around a Democrat and have to listen to his spiel. In today's world, there is a huge gap. I am anti-abortion, pro-traditional family with a father and a mother, and I want to keep my guns, and have a strong military. I de-friend Democrats I don't want to hear or see!

You can't de-friend a staff person.

But we get ourselves into unpleasant staff relations in the camp setting in the name of Christian charity. She needs a job so I can overlook her position on drinking alcohol. He has a nice family and I know his mom and dad, so I won't dig too deep to find out what type of worker he really has been at other jobs. She talks about preaching while on camp visits to churches, but the camp's denomination does not hire lady preachers. The list can go on and on. We compromise in the name of desperation. We compromise out of charity.

You can compromise and let a younger camper come to a camp that his mother insists he is ready to attend. You can compromise and give a refund even when your policy says, "no refunds." You can't compromise whom and what you hire.

I recently read how the CEO of Charles Schwab finds out if a new hire will make a great fit within his company. He takes the interviewee out for breakfast, but beforehand he tells the restaurant manager to mess up the order. He wants to see how the new hire will react, how he will treat the wait staff, and he wants to see if he is too meek and mild to say anything. Not a bad technique at all, I would say– he is finding out the true character of the interviewee and it is costing him only a 20 dollar bill.

Really, really understand the character of your new hire. Everyone looks great on paper. The resume is not a barometer of character, only the thermometer of what a staff has done and how long they have done it. Thermometers tell what and barometers tell how. I want to know the how of a person: how did he accomplish assignments at his former job, how did he interact with other staff, how did he finish a job, and how much was he missed by the employees on the last job. (If no one is missing him – that should say something to you!)

After 31 years here at the same camp, it has not been the lack of money, the lack of business, the lack of equipment or time that has caused me the most heartache and headaches. It has always been the bad hires. Dealing with bad hires will take the love of work away from you. And you, as a new director of a camp, sure don't need to go through that in the first five years. You need unity and peace and a workforce that is team-oriented

Yep, the statement is true: "hire slower, fire faster." My prayer is that you do hire slow enough...so that there will not be the need to fire.

CHAPTER 21
Work Life Balance

Human beings are complex energy systems, and full engagement is not simply one-dimensional. The energy that pulses through us is physical, emotional, mental, and spiritual. All four dynamics are critical, none is sufficient by itself and each profoundly influences the others. To perform at our best, we must skillfully manage each of these interconnected dimensions of energy. Subtract any one from the equation and our capacity to fully ignite our talent and skill is diminished, much the way an engine sputters when one of its cylinders misfires.

Jim Loehr; Tony Schwartz - *The Power of Full Engagement: Managing Energy, Not Time, is the Key to High Performance and Personal Renewal*

I remember in 1991 stopping by to pick up toner for our office copier and sharing with the owner, Don, how weary I was feeling. I had been the director of a brand new camp for just over three years. I was shorthanded to the point that I was even ordering the food and planning the menus for the weekend retreats. I was facing burnout.

It so happened that Don had a son-in-law who was a cook at another Christian camp in Indiana and was wanting to get back closer to family. Within three months, I was not picking up groceries anymore. I shared my weariness, Don heard, and the Lord opened the doors for a new cook to come on staff.

If you haven't felt this way yet, hold on. You will hit the wall. You will be so near burnout that you mind turns to fuzz. You will wake up one morning with no desire to keep going. Only the noise of your children playing in the next room will drive you back to your job again, knowing that they need fed.

If you are in your first camp director's role, you have much to learn. The culture, the layout, the staff, the finances, the churches, and systems. You have spent the last year just trying to put it all together into something understandable called "managing the camp." You're the main dog, and everyone around appears to have a big heavy chain attached to your collar. Pulled here. Yanked there. There is no time to actually sit down and put together a coherent plan.

I remember a friend who was a maintenance man at a neighboring camp. The camp was slightly understaffed, but adequate. My friend and his family came into the camp without any camp experience, but extremely excited about working in an outdoor setting. Both the husband and wife worked at camp. He was maintenance and she cooked weekends and throughout the summer. They lasted about three years. She was a good cook and he was a jack of all trades and did maintenance pretty well. What happened?

They lost control from the beginning. This family had five young daughters with mom and dad both engaged very deeply in the day-to-day operation of the camp. It sucked their life from them.

Their thinking became fuzzy and they spiraled downward from then on. There was no management of work time and off time – it became a mental 80 hour a week job.

When we started working in camps, my wife stayed home and cared for our four children; she also home schooled them. Eventually, she filtered into working full-time, but only after the kids were well into their teen years. If I could advise a new director with children one thing, I would encourage him to let mom stay home and be mom; she will help keep life balanced when camp is running at a hundred miles an hour.

I like what Brian Howard writes about simple steps to avoid burnout:

"Every day take four hours off. Every day, take at least four hours and get away from your work. I encourage leaders to look at a week as 21 four-hour time blocks. Each day has three time blocks: 8-12, 1-5 and 6-10. **Take one of these time blocks every day and do nothing that is related to your work.** *Exercise, spend time with your family, play or watch a sport, hang out with friends, take a walk, pay attention to your soul. But whatever you do, stop working. Daily rest is critical. If on a particular day or two you don't get rest, make sure to prioritize it today. You can't work very many 12-hour days and avoid collapse."*

As I visit camps and get to know a director, I listen to what he says about how many hours he is working each week. When I hear him say 80+ hours, I know he is just months from quitting or worse yet, being fired due to lack of performance. I have worked in two camps over the past 37 years, and I can count on one hand the number of **actual** 80 hour weeks I have put in. Emphasis on actual.

"But you don't understand," you are saying. "I am the only one here and if I don't keep my nose to the grindstone and work seven days a week, the camp will cease to exist." My answer to that statement would be, "Then let it die. Better it, than you." Nothing, and I mean nothing, is worth killing yourself off for. Playing the role of a martyr worked for just a few, and even then, those few were killed because of their testimony for Christ. No one was martyred for mowing, or cleaning, or cooking or producing brochures. If you do want to have your life burned at a stake or stoned to death, then be martyred for the right reason.

Much of camp is physical. There are buildings and plates and grass and horses and sewer pumps and roads and playgrounds and schedules. All great stuff that needs managed and organized. If you don't pay attention to these things, pretty soon people will stop coming down your gravel road. Pretty soon you can become a has-been camp that used to be great. The pressure is on to stay after all elements of the camp; to be on top of all things.

And then there is the spiritual. The ministry side of camp IS the reason we exist as Christian camps. We exist so that others may come to know Christ, to be strengthened in their faith, and to be built up and trained to be witnesses to others of salvation through the Savior– Jesus.

New directors can get out of balance quite quickly if they are not careful. Too much emphasis on buildings can leave the ministry side of camp weak and ineffective. Too much time spent on developing programs and curriculum can leave a camp a run-down place that is not attractive to those who want to attend the great programs.

Camp life is all about balance. Balance of time. Balance of priorities. Balance of emphasis. It is not that a director can't be focused fully on a new building for nine months. He must be the pusher on the project. But after nine months, he has to come back to the office and look at the programs and spend the next few months on just reworking the program. The same with personnel; maybe a director uses only the slower months of January and February to emphasize extensive staff training to full-time staff.

Camp runs in rhythms. There are intense times. There are slow times. There are times of snow and there is a time for grass. There are holidays and then there is summer camp. Each has its own intensity or lack of intensity. By quickly understanding the rhythms of camp, it helps a director to anticipate the breaks. Our staff knows that from Labor Day until Thanksgiving it is push, push, push. And then we have November 25 to January 3 – ah, the joy of downtime. A director who anticipates and then keeps communicating this will keep staff working harder and longer knowing that downtime is just ahead.

CHAPTER 22

Drive it Home to Done

"I believe in simplicity. It is astonishing as well as sad, how many trivial affairs even the wisest thinks he must attend to in a day; so simplify the problem of life, distinguish the necessary and the real."

Henry David Thoreau

Ideas are fun to generate. Plans are even more fun to plan. Implementation is another thing completely; implementation means work, focus, sweat, and a pit-bull mentality that grabs hold of an idea and drives it to done – to completion – to reality.

In our world filled with ADHD-type symptoms, compelled by too many video type games that create a virtual world of excitement at the push of a button, staying on focus is difficult work. We like our distractions.

And if you are in a smaller camp, distractions abound.

Twenty years ago, I was a distracted director. I did the marketing, the promotions, I mowed the grass, watched the budget, swept up after a retreat, baled hay, trucked in donations, and tried to have the appearance of being in charge of the organization. My life was distracted.

Today it is different. I am writing this book while the rest of the staff works preparing for the weekend and for the summer ministry. I literally could be gone for weeks and everything would function just as well.

However, that is not where you are today; otherwise you would not be reading this and trying to figure out how you can become a leader others would follow. You would not be wanting to grow and mature into a more effective leader of your camp.

There are many sought-after attributes that help create a successful director— a director who is easy to follow: kind, empathetic, team player, and one with integrity. All those are important as you interact with staff and lead.

But leading an organization takes another set of attributes. Perseverance, grit, tenacity, and focus are key elements. For me, tenacity and focus have given me the ability and the drive to finish what I said I would do. It drives the project to done.

Whether it is a new program, a new building, a new retreat, it is the ability of locking in like a bird dog on a covey of quail and staying locked on until every bird is flushed. And it means staying with it without delegating it to someone else.

I love delegation. I am considered a master of delegation by the camp staff. I don't hold on to things that other staff can do as well or better than me. However, when it is something new, I will not hand it off until it is done and there are some elementary systems in place to get it running and going in the right direction.

An example. We built the Family Life Center... 27,000 square foot recreation building complete with gym, indoor pool, game room, sleeping rooms, and large central foyer with snack areas. We created the dream in the 90's but didn't begin on the project until 2006. I drove it. I worked shoulder to shoulder with our staff builder and other staff. I was there before everyone else in the morning and I was the last one to turn out the lights at the end of the day. I planned staff's responsibilities, I managed volunteers, and I protected our actual builder from interruptions. We were occupying the building within seven months from digging the foundation.

Had I not driven the project, it would not have been completed in time for our winter groups to use it. Once completed, I backed off. However, during that time I was deeply engaged in building, many other things went undone by me. Concentrated focus meant that I concentrated on the **most** important thing at that time. I concentrated on the one thing that would influence the camp for years in the future.

The results: our retreat business doubled within two years, creating a more healthy cash flow. For the first time in years, we were able to weather the slower winter months; we had enough cash to pay for salaries, do remodeling projects, buy summer program equipment and actually feel we were in control of our finances.

Do I commit as much energy and focus to all projects? No. Not all projects we do impact the business like I knew the Family Life Center would. I am tenacious when it actually matters. We have done other buildings and I was only mildly interested or involved. We have other staff who can drive smaller projects home.

The key is to know how important the results of any project are to the health and stability of the camp; if it is vital, do it yourself. If there are marginal results or returns, then delegate it to others. Know when only you can get the job done.

CHAPTER 23

The Metric that Matters

Be it a politician or someone working in a company, perhaps the most valuable thing we can do if we are to truly serve our constituents is to know them personally. It would be impossible to know all of them, but to know the name and details of the life of someone we are trying to help with our product, service or policy makes a huge difference. The moment we are able to make tangible that which had previously been a study or a chart, the moment a statistic or a poll becomes a real living person, the moment abstract concepts are understood to have human consequences, is the moment our ability to solve problems and innovate becomes remarkable.

Simon Sinek - *Leaders Eat Last:
Why Some Teams Pull Together and Others Don't*

It is about the people and not the numbers. For those of us whose eyes glass over when it comes time to work with analytical numbers– there is hope. I keep track of numbers that matter: is there money in the checkbook, is there money in reserve, is there enough business scheduled for the upcoming year. These are the dashboard figures that matter to me.

I have nothing against those who need and use complicated systems to track and project the successes and failures of their camp. I honestly tried to understand a bigger system; however, it didn't come natural to me, which, in turn, meant I soon forgot it and went back to my old ways.

There are many things you need to keep track of as the director of the camp; reality says you had better understand your income and expenses or you won't have a job for long. The system you use needs to make sense to you and your bookkeeper. There are complicated systems that only finance-type of people will understand and there is something as simple as QuickBooks, that even I can get.

There will be CPA-type of people who will want you to understand the finances of your camp on their level: this is impossible. Don't even go there. I personally have told our CPA who audits our books, "Your end of the year report makes no sense to me and I would not use it in my decision-making process." Does that mean her work is useless? No. It just means MY head cannot wrap itself around things like depreciation, total net worth, or unrestricted net assets.

Church Mutual and other insurance companies want their year-end report of the number of camper days, number of boats, number of horses, and if you have a zip line or a climbing wall. They want hard facts that they can put into their computers to compute your insurance rate for the next year. I figure the camper days begrudgingly; I find the numbers of no value otherwise. I hear and read about the number of camper days other camps are experiencing: "28,000 camper days – up from 22,000 last year" are the headlines the director declares. So? What does that mean? I guess you could assume growth from the increase in numbers. I assume you can make a comparison to other camps and understand the size of their influence by these figures. I only see them as Church Mutual numbers.

Is that heresy? Probably. But for me, they don't mean a thing. An effective leader deals with the important things. The important things that will make a difference on the bottom line or in people's lives.

If you are new to a director's position, you will be inundated by many different aspects of the camp you have to keep track of and record properly. There's income. There's expenses. There are construction costs and projections. There is anticipating the amount of business and the amount of revenue from retreats. There is gift income from friends of the camp. There are hourly salaries to track. There are food costs. There is overhead and fixed cost of operating a camp with or without guests. It all can become overwhelming in the first 18 months as you try to get a handle on the financial health of your camp.

To keep it simple, I would only focus on a couple things initially. How do this year's finances compare to last year's? And have we spent less than we have taken in? Pretty basic stuff that the non-financially minded person can grasp.

Why is a previous year's comparison so important? It helps you see if there is growth with income and it shows you where your expenses are steady and where expenses are wildly fluctuating and out of control. I personally view this two or three times a month as I am making financial decisions for the future. I need to know this information so that I can decide if we can actually afford a new blob for this year– perhaps in light of having higher food and energy cost, but not increased revenue, I will have to say no to the blob for now. Previous year reports created by QuickBooks are a great tool for building next year's budget as well. You should be able to see some type of pattern in income and spending with two or more years of actual figures in front of you.

You can spend enormous amounts of time trying to break down cost per plate and cost per bed. You can try to come up with a figure that depicts the actual cost of summer camp. You can pour over these numbers and come up with an estimated cost; it may not be the actual cost.

Let me give you an example. After last summer, our summer ministry team declared that they actually made money from summer camp. I was quite shocked to hear this; I had always known that summer camp costs us money to operate. I asked them, "How did you come up with THAT?" They replied, "We took the amount of money spent under summer camp expenses and compared it to the income from summer camp." I smiled at their simplistic approach. "Did you factor in insurance, full-time year-round staff, new construction costs, electricity, water, propane, and equipment to run summer camp like mowers and chainsaws?" "No," they said sheepishly. I said, "Then you did not make money!"

Do you see how it is nearly impossible to come up with an actual dollar amount for summer camp? How much time do you allocate from staff salaries to summer camp? These staff have worked all year long preparing for summer camp, all the while doing retreats and keeping the buildings and grounds clean and updated. At best, you can ball-park a number for summer camp which can then help you set next year's fees.

I can hear old time directors "clicking their tongues" at me for suggesting this. Remember, I am writing for young and new directors who need some quick advice to get them through their first three to five years. It takes time to create metrics that matter.

It takes time to sort out the important elements of which statistic or numbers actually matter in the long run.

Today, I am much more interested in many different things about our camp. I do track utility usage. I do track food costs. I am interested in percent of returning retreat groups. I want to know what percentage of retreat groups are youth and college age kids in comparison to family campers. Knowing these facts helps me make decisions about how buildings are built, what amenities we include in the buildings, and how we market and communicate with our current users. I have <u>grown</u> to need extra metrics as the camp has grown. If I were in a smaller camp, and just starting out, I would worry about the bottom line – do we have enough income to pay the bills – which should spur a director on to begin writing letters, visiting churches, or beginning a marketing plan to increase usage. Whenever there is a money shortage, action should soon follow.

I do keep a close watch on the finances of the camp; without enough money, the camp begins to flounder and morale and facilities go downhill. Staff likes to be paid. But I have an even more important system to measure the success of the camp: it is called my "happiness file."

In my desk, I keep a file of all the good reports I hear from parents, churches, and campers. In it are testimonies that talk about the influence of the camp on a child or family's lives. It is the letter from a mother who writes about her daughter who came to camp with an attitude that showed disrespect, but returned home willing and ready to accept the parent's authority in her life. It is the letters from a church pastor telling about a family who was near divorce, but having attended family camp, returned home and reconciled and started anew. It is the testimony from the 40-year-old man who explains it took two trips to camp, but during a men's retreat he accepted Christ in one of our dining rooms.

My simple advice: do keep track of the money. Know where your money is spent. Don't be in a hurry to break things down to the nth degree just yet. Watch the bottom line and the checkbook balance. But most important, rejoice that you are making a difference in children's lives. This is the metric that matters first; this will propel you to work harder and later in order to see real fruit for your labors.

CHAPTER 24

No More Meetings

Give meeting participants something tangible— an agenda or specific goals— that you can all use to keep yourselves on track. Do this by communicating to participants— two days before a meeting, if you can— the purpose of the discussion and what you hope to resolve. Then, when you open the meeting, remind people of the goals by saying something like this: "What do we want to have decided, determined, discovered, or declared dead at the end of this meeting?"

Robert M. Galford; Bob Frisch; Cary Greene -
Simple Sabotage: A Modern Field Manual for Detecting and Rooting Out Everyday Behaviors That Undermine Your Workplace

Do not have more meetings, but better meetings. How do you know when you are in a meeting chasing a rabbit trail? When you start seeing rabbit pellets.

We exist in a church culture that wants meetings. For staff, it means an hour with donuts and coffee. It means an hour away from the phone or off the tractor. It is down time.

I personally believe that meetings should be such difficult work that no one looks forward to them; they all know they are going to have to think, discuss real issues, and make decisions. There are other types of meetings – I call them gab sessions that end up with nothing accomplished. I don't do those meetings. I save that for over the lunch hour.

Staff meetings have two functions. One function is to inform, communicate, and encourage staff in their work. Weekend schedules could be discussed. Issues that are affecting the entire staff might be talked over.

However, the office staff does not care about the problems of the maintenance staff unless it affects them. Don't bring all the staff together to discuss all of the camp problems – if it deals with maintenance – have a maintenance meeting. If the office phones were acting wacky and something needs to be done about a new system, bring in the office gals who work with the phones; kitchen staff doesn't need to be involved in call waiting decisions.

When the wrong people attend the wrong staff meetings, rabbit pellets begin to appear. Time is wasted.

For years I was frustrated with our Thursday staff meeting. Everyone was there. There was plenty of yackety-yack, but I could not move the conversation into a strategy/planning session. I wanted to do some long-range thinking, and the staff just wanted to discuss dishwasher malfunctions or lack of grass for the horses. I finally solved the problem.

I now have two different staff meetings. One with lead staff who thinks big picture and the other staff meeting discusses operational issues. And I only invite those who have a stake in the decision-making process. We are productive and at the end of the meeting we accomplish what we set to do; and there are no rabbit pellets.

However, I don't have meetings weekly unless needed. If there is nothing on the agenda, then we don't meet. If I need to communicate something, an email works just fine for details. Meetings should not be used for disseminating details, meetings should be used to discuss ideas and plans. If you are using your Thursday staff meetings to review assignments for the weekend, you are wasting a good hour. Type up assignments, hand them out and expect people to be there on the weekend and be early. No discussion needed. That is an administrative responsibility that needs to be handled in the office by the retreat director.

Meetings are necessary for training. We use our paid lunch hour to hold staff training sessions throughout the winter. We watch a video, discuss an idea found in a book, or we have a hands-on demonstration. By doing it over the lunch hour you maximize everyone's time and because everybody loves to eat… you have 100% participation.

However, if you are meeting and all you end up with is a pile of rabbit pellets, you might want to re-imagine what your meetings could look like.

CHAPTER 25

Working with Your Board

"Boards need to understand basic strategy,
but it's not their job to create it."

Ram Charan -
Owning Up: The 14 Questions Every Board Member
Needs to Ask

Most camp boards are made of men and women who truly love the ministry. They might have attended your camp or worked as a counselor at your camp. They might have had children work at your camp. There is an unusually close relationship. However the camp board is completely different than the normal church board.

Church board members return to church every Sunday and probably during the week as well. They have constant contact with the pastor and they have constant interaction with those who attend church. They feel and hear the continuous heartbeat of the church.

Not so with the camp board members. Camp board members may at best attend a men's or women's retreat or perhaps bring their family to a summer family camp. They may just drop off a child for a week of camp. They then return home, leaving the camp staff to carry on the business of camp without their direct oversight. Their four to six board meetings per year may be on-site, but not always.

Many young camp directors accept their responsibilities with an assumption that the camp board will function like the church board. It doesn't, it won't, and if it does, you have big problems as the director. Most small church boards are permission granting boards; you don't want that type of board at your camp. If you have to wait for your quarterly board meeting to get permission to move ahead with an idea or a new program, you lose momentum and time. Execution of ideas needs feet to run in order to become reality; feet movement is fed by emotion and urgency. Boards can sometime cripple action by shuffling a decision off to a committee to discuss it further. Once it moves into a committee, the idea becomes either dead or so muddled with the committee's input that it is unrecognizable.

How does a new director reshape how a camp board functions without over-stepping his role? And a dictator-type of director is not good either.

If I had to do it all over again, I would do the following things with even more regularity than I did as a young director:

1) I would over-communicate my thoughts– not with wordy prose that ends up filling five or six pages. I would follow the politician's playbook and regularly communicate bullet points that are written as statements rather than as questions. A couple examples might be:

- Pump blew up in well house – replaced pump with a $3000 rebuilt motor.

- Staff attending CCCA conference – conference will cost camp $120 per person – a great value.
- Moving ahead with the design of new girls' cabins – will begin fund-raising once a floor plan and exterior design are complete.

With this type of bullet point communication, you lay out intentions. You lead. You develop the ideas. You create the vision. You control the timing rather than waiting for a board to grant permission.

You build trust by completing ideas and projects that you bullet point out! If you are a young director, the board has no idea if you can deliver the goods. You looked good on paper. Your resume is solid, maybe even epic. However, until you are put into a game, the board is still looking at you as a rookie who will make rookie mistakes. Until you have scored 4 touchdowns in one game or led a last minute 80 yard drive to win the game, they are looking at you as suspect.

2) I would ensure that I create some immediate wins by delivering on promises. I would make sure that my ideas are accomplishable. There is nothing more damaging to the trust of a new director than when he says, "I will accomplish building new buildings, rework old programs, remodel all the cabins, and hire the greatest staff ever amassed at one camp." Slow your rhetoric down to doable sound bites. "I will hire ten staff by March 1. I will rework the wilderness program so that it will be more challenging and attractive to the 10-year-old boy. I will train all full-time staff during the month of February." Make sure your to-do list is measurable so you can report back in future sound bites to the board, "10 staff are hired. Secured outdoor cooking equipment and canoes for wilderness boys. Staff has had 4 weeks of

training using principles found in Danny Meyer's book *"Setting the Table."* You win the board's trust one success at a time.

3) I would come better prepared for the board meeting with complete understanding of the finances. If I were passing out a previous year's comparison expenditure and income sheet to the board, I would want to know why we spent $3000 more this year under the line item of maintenance equipment. I would want to know the exact reason we spent the money and be able to articulate the value of the purchase. Young directors get blind-sided by well-meaning board members who are bean-counters and sticklers when it comes to budgets and finances. It is the job of the board to oversee the financial positions and well-being of the camp; if a new director even appears that she does not know the details of expenditures – trust is broken. Once trust is broken – then micromanagement by the board sets in. I would say this could be the most important aspect of a young director's success with working with a board – know where your income is coming from, and most importantly – know where you are spending the dollars. Once you have the deer-in-the-headlights look regarding the finances of the camp – you are setting your-self up for pain inflicted by the board. Your board will no longer be your friendly advisor – they will become your overseer.

4) I would become better friends with board members. Board members are not ogres sitting under bridges waiting for you to screw up. Board members do want the best for the director and the camp; that is why they hired you. I would try to get to know their families in non-board situations. I would stop and visit their homes or their work. I would hope I can become a friend.

5) I would make sure all new board members are brought up to speed on as many details as possible with copies of minutes from the previous year. I would make sure they had copies of all my

written reports from the previous years. If you have a staff policy manual, I would make sure they had a copy. If you have a detailed manual of all policies that the board has made, they should see that as well.

By creating a new board member packet of information, a new board member knows what has been hot items over the past year. He will see patterns with the financial reports. He can read about the concerns of other board members regarding programs or people. Board meetings are an accumulation of all past board meetings: all policies, all decisions, all new programs need to be understood before making new decisions. You want new decisions to build off former policies and not to create conflict and lack of clarity.

As I visit with camp directors, there appears to be a lack of understanding on the director's role in relationship to individuals on the board. At times there is an overreach by some board members that confuses new camp directors. New camp directors feel pressured when one board member tries to push his agenda on the director while not in an official board meeting. A tug of war ensues and usually someone leaves a bit mad and bloody. Many board members do not understand or live by the motto: "When we are adjourned, we are totally adjourned." Board members who believe it is their duty to continue being a board member outside the boardroom usually become a nemesis to a new director.

I write a welcome letter to new board members that explains some of the processes and former decisions the board has made. This is included in the new board member introductory packet that is received prior to their first board meeting. I discuss the role of the board and I discuss how some rogue board members try to influence and make decisions outside the board meeting. I try to show them how destructive that type of board member can become. Board members are coming onto the camp board after serving their local church board; they think they will govern the same way as they do back home. Retrain, retrain, and retrain.

The relationship between the board and the director evolves. Figure your first year to be a strain. They need to test you. They need to see if you are grasping the culture. Figure you will be micromanaged. However, you cannot let this behavior become the standard operating procedure. You have to break the bad habits of the board and you do this only one way. Deliver results. Deliver understandable reports that make sense and show you have a grasp on the condition of the finances. Finish what you say you are going to do. Develop a systematic written report to the board prior to the board meeting. Give the board time, prior to the board meeting, to digest and ruminate over the plans and observations you plan to discuss regarding personnel, finance, program, and development. Use the same template with every board report: all reports should look the same from board meeting to board meeting. Remember, you work with this information every day, but a board member looks at it four times each year. Keep it simple, clear, and don't ask questions. Instead, project ideas, plans, and your solutions to current problems.

Create an open relationship with your board chairman. Board chairmen are the leaders of the board. They have been appointed or elected because either they are skilled leaders or they have been around the camp board for so long they know all the details of the camp. I personally have had board chairmen who were great leaders but lacked understanding on how the camp works. I have had other chairmen who were the biggest cheerleaders available but were not the strong, take charge leader. Personally, I would take the cheerleader any day over the strong personality. Regardless, you need to know what type of chairman you have and then adjust how you work with each one. Once you destroy or damage your relationship with the chairman you can figure on your board meetings becoming your most stressful day of the quarter: you will dread them.

Boards are placed over a director to help her see big picture issues. They are available as a sounding board. They are there to protect and prevent disaster from occurring to the camp. They watch the health of the finances. They ensure proper insurance policies are in place. They see that staff salaries and benefits are adequate. But don't assume the board will create vision for the camp.

I personally have been frustrated about working with the board on strategic thinking. I have tried and I have failed. What starts off as trying to develop long-range plans dissolves into hearing eight different perspectives about camp. The perspectives range from comments like this:

- "We are doing great… better than last year."
- "I think we need to bring in go carts and paint ball and build a 1000 foot zip line across the ravine."
- "We need more staff but we should pay them as little as possible with no insurance."
- "Let's not build anymore and just stay the same. It costs too much money."

Ideas are all over the place. There is no logic in their perspective, only preferences. There is usually no research on the needs of the churches, only their opinions.

It is the director's job to set the course. It is the director's job to lay out a comprehensive strategy that contains potential buildings and a plan that includes programs and people needed to run the programs. However, it is also the director's job to engage and expect the board to be a blessing in return. According to John Pearson in his blog www.ecfagovernance.blogspot.com (I highly recommend subscribing to this!):

> "You're driving away from a 'typical' board meeting (or sharing the experience with a friend or family member), and you say, 'THAT WAS A GREAT BOARD MEETING TODAY!' Tell me, what happened at the board meeting to provoke that positive response?"

- Over the years, when I ask this question, board members with unsatisfactory experiences often respond:
    - "No one asked me for advice, wisdom, counsel or ideas."
    - "The staff read the reports that all of us had read in advance."
    - "Boring. Routine. Pure agony."
    - "Clearly, I'm not needed at the board table. The CEO did all the talking."
    - "There was no sense of the holy, except the perfunctory bookend prayers."
- Conversely—here's what highly committed, deeply engaged, thrilled-to-be-serving board members tell me:
    - "Everyone's prepared. Everyone participates. Everyone prays. It's the best board I have ever served on!"
    - "It happens all the time! We've deleted the petty stuff and focus on the important agenda items only. And...we're on target financially."

- *One board member outlined four primary ingredients of memorable board meetings:*
  1. *There is deep joy—consistently in every meeting.*
  2. *The board is focused on strategic issues.*
  3. *Energetic discussions abound! "We're not looking for agreement—we're looking for insight. Spiritual insight."*
  4. *There is solidarity. "We foster a board culture that eliminates the unhealthy giving up of personal beliefs for the sake of unity. Instead, we wait for the Spirit of God to speak."*

How would your board members describe the last board meeting at your camp? How can you as the director create an atmosphere where board members will use such phrases as "pure joy" or "we waited for the Spirit of God to speak" when they talk about serving on the camp board?

I had a board member back in the '80's who was a gem. She was full of ideas about new programs. She declared at every board meeting the need to develop a full-blown year-round horse program. I loved her vision and her spunk, but she was forgetting a couple important elements in her declaration. We would need some type of building and we would need a person to run this dream of hers. I was in my third year as the director, and I became a bit confused about her expectations, but I also held my ground and said, "Some day." Some day came, and now we have a horse program complete with two part-time horse staff, 30 horses, two barns, 25 acres of pasture, and 40 acres of hay ground. If we had reacted to her ideas and her persuasion, we might have started something we could not have finished well.

When the director and staff develop the long-range strategy for the camp, it is done with understanding and with realistic questions about each component. Returning to the horse program idea from the board member. Great idea, but she had not considered the big picture. *How much would this cost? Are we willing to take good farm ground out of production to grow grass and hay? Is there anyone who can be trained or has an interest in horses? What will insurance cost for each horse? Is there a demand by campers? Do people really ride horses in the snow and cold?* Staff can flesh out these questions. Staff can put together a plan for a future horse program complete with costs, staffing needs and projected income to be presented to the board to agree or disagree.

Young directors, do yourself a favor and come to the board prepared with a plan and do not expect them to come up with the plan. It is their job to discuss your plan and feel comfortable with voting either yes or no. It is their job to suggest revisions or evaluate your thoroughness. It is not their job to come up with strategic ideas or plans. Coming prepared with a plan is faster, more precise, and usually, you will be able to move ahead quickly on implementation of your plan.

And… you will own the plan, which means you will be more personally invested. You will see that it gets driven to complete. And then you will have your win with the board, you will build their trust, and you can return again with the next BIG IDEA!

CHAPTER 26

My Story - Dick Angelo

*Some of my first encounters with Dick were during
workshops that he led. After attending the first one, I always
attended any that he led in future years. His quiet, Spirit-
led demeanor was a balm to my soul. He not only knew
how to create and direct a camp, he knew how to do it with
a total dependence on the Lord. Camp Forest Springs is a
wonderful teaching camp that is being used by six different
colleges to send their camping majors to do a year of
internship in Camp Forest Spring's Leadership, Training,
and Development program.dick@forestsprings.org*

(Authors Note)

Just as King David had a lot to learn in his youthful years, I had a
lot to learn during my first ten years in Christian camping. As God
used Saul to show David how not to be king, so God used many
experiences in my early years to show me how not to treat people,
how not to administer and lead, and how to trust God by faith.

The greatest character development that I can reflect on is how
to trust God by faith. This is done by being able to let God be

the director of the camp, while allowing Him to work through me to administer the daily, weekly, and yearly functions of the camp.

My leadership brought in a strong emphasis on the following two areas:

- At the board level – to operate as a strong policy board

- At the administrative level – to lead from a servant-leadership concept

A distinction was made between a policy board versus an operational board. Some of the distinctions include:

Policy Board	Operational Board
– Delegate to director to set schedule for the camp	– Board sets schedule and plans out the year
– Staff employees develop the budget and bring to the board to approve or change	– Board sets budget
– CEO is a visionary planner, has administrative gifts and thinks as a director long-range.	– CEO tends to be a manager, wanting to carry out the board decisions
– Board meeting centers around approving, discussing policy, and giving direction to the CEO to administer the camps	– Board tends to spend a lot of time in meeting planning schedule and program, selecting speakers, and planning details of camp operation
– Meetings tend to be less frequent and shorter	– Meetings tend to be more frequent and longer
– Board tends to be made up of more professionally skilled members	– Board tends to be made up of more pastors and blue collar members

When a board is able to spend their time with policy and the staff cares for the operation of the camp, the board is able to deal more effectively with long-range planning, is able to move the camp ahead more quickly, and be much more involved in the total large picture for the future.

A culture that we are still developing is that of a servant leadership style of leadership. There are a number of times when Jesus talked to His disciples about leadership and said:

- Be different – don't lead like the Gentiles
- Don't lord it over others
- Be willing to serve
- Example of washing the feet of His disciples

A quick overview of the culture at Forest Springs is to operate in the following way:

- The organization writes the ministry description vs. the employee writing it.
- The immediate supervisor trains the employee completely in the position, so they clearly understand the ministry description.
- During the training time (may be as long as six months to a year or more), the supervisor gives the employee a balance between authority and responsibility. It is very important that those two aspects are kept in balance as the two individuals go through the process. At the time that the supervisor feels the employee fully understands the role they play, then full responsibility and full authority is handed over to the employee.

- With that done, now the role of a servant steps in. The supervisor now, so to speak, goes under the employee and spends the rest of their time helping the employee become as successful as possible.

So much happens between the supervisor and the employee at this point, resulting in the following:

- Creates unity. John 17: 22-23 – *"And the glory which Thou has given Me I have given to them; that they may be one, just as We are one; I in them, and Thou in Me, that they may be perfected in unity, that the world may know that Thou didst send Me, and didst love them, even as Thou didst love Me."*

- Develops love for one another. John 15: 12 – *"This is My commandment, that you love one another, just as I have loved you."*

- Eliminates jealousy and selfishness. James 3: 14-16 – *"But if you have bitter jealousy and selfish ambition in your heart, do not be arrogant and so lie against the truth. This wisdom is not that which comes down from above, but is earthly, natural, demonic. For where jealousy and selfish ambition exist, there is disorder and every evil thing."*

- Allows no place for disorder and evil. James 3: 14-16 (same as above).

- Eliminates reasons to be jealous of workers because the leader's goal is to make the workers look good and help them become leaders.

- Eliminates strife. Philippians 2: 3 – *"Do nothing from selfishness or empty conceit, but with humility of mind let each of you regard one another as more important than himself."*

- Strengthens individuals – does not weaken them.
- Desires the best for another person – isn't that just like God?

WHAT YOUNG DIRECTORS SHOULD CONCENTRATE ON

Our world culture is so strong on having us know the correct management style, the latest ideas in leadership, and the best human contacts to have. As leaders we tend to chase all of those ideas and concepts. How many times have we been asked, "What books have you most recently read?" It seems that the answer to that question positions our relationship with those who are around us in leadership.

The question I want to ask is, "If God, Jehovah, Jesus, Who created us and we believe we are created in His image, and if He left His written Word for each of us to use to guide our lives, then why shouldn't my first answer to the question about what book I have recently read be the Bible? I should be saying I just don't get enough time to study His Word in order to get direction for my leadership role.

The best practice that a young or old director can get into is to take all the cares of the week, make a list of them, and daily spend time in prayer over them. Keep that list at least a week ahead all the time. That way, one prays for the needs of today, as well as always praying for the needs of the next several days.

Did I know what size of a camp or the kind of a camp program I wanted when I became director? The answer is no. Over the forty years of my director/president role, I continually asked God to guide us, keep us from making mistakes, and give wisdom for the future to the camp staff and board of directors. One great guideline is to look to your leadership around you and ask God to direct all of you by common sense and faith.

Now faith– that is another subject. Hebrews 11: 1a says, *"Now faith is being sure of what we hope for and certain of what we do not see."*

One guiding principle that I have always kept before the board and the staff is that in all of our development projects, my prayer has been, *"Lord, don't bring a millionaire into our midst to underwrite the project. Please cause us to take steps of faith with You so we learn to trust You, so we know what it's like to see Your hand on the project, and so that we never transfer our trust from You, Lord, to human beings. Lord, protect us from a proud spirit of what we have done, lest we forget that You did it."*

HOW GOD PREPARED ME FOR MY CAMP LEADERSHIP EXPERIENCE

I grew up in a Christian home, attended a church that preached the gospel and was part of a denomination that operated two camps.

At about the age of 12, my mother asked me if I had ever accepted Christ as Savior. At that time, I said no, but I wasn't ready to do that then. She proceeded to ask me if I want to. I said, "yes," knowing that it would be over in her mind and she would not bother me anymore. So, we prayed together, but I didn't mean a thing I said.

For the next four years, the Holy Spirit worked in my life. I had a conviction that I covered up. I knew all the answers to salvation and faked my life as a "Christian."

I spent a week at church camp. I was ready to pray and accept Christ, but for several reasons, I didn't want to do it by myself. I looked for someone to pray with. I remember going around camp looking for someone to talk with me about salvation. I went to the waterfront one morning, into the kitchen one day, spent time hanging around my counselor, but no one ever asked or talked to me about salvation.

At the age of 16, I went forward in a special evangelistic meeting after the speaker asked, "If you die tonight, do you know you will go to Heaven?"

After high school, I attended college for two years, taking general subjects. Then, I attended technical college for two years, got married (still married for 52 years), became a licensed airplane mechanic, and worked for several years for a major airline. During that time, I also took training in finances at a business college.

During my college years, I spent each summer in Christian camps, serving as a lifeguard, counselor, recreation leader, and unit leader. While working for the airline, the founder and director of Camp Forest Springs (now Forest Spring Camp and Conference Center) asked my wife and I to join staff full-time. We joined staff in 1966 as the program director. Ten years later, I became the director and now serve as president.

During my ten years as program director, I finished my college undergrad with a teaching degree in physical education, minoring in psychology and completed a masters degree in leadership/administration.

My camp experiences during those years formed so much of my camping leadership philosophy, in particular my camp salvation experience. Because of that, I built into the program I was responsible for a concept called "one-on-one." I wanted every camper to leave camp having the opportunity to be one-on-one with the counselor. It has become one of the strongholds of my camping experience over the past 30+ years.

Also during the summer, all of our staff are challenged at some time with their personal relationship with Jesus, knowing how one can have all the answers and yet not be a true child of God.

Over and above my college and graduate training, my aviation training was some of the most helpful to me during the time of becoming the director in 1976. We were in a total redevelopment of the camp and I had to communicate with architects, plumbers, electricians, and contractors. I could speak the technical language of all the trades due to the background God gave me in the aviation industry.

It became so clear to me that God does not make mistakes. If one is willing to give one's life to God, as in Romans 12: 1-2, *"Therefore, I urge you, brothers, in view of God's mercy, to offer your bodies as living sacrifices, holy and pleasing to God – this is your spiritual act of worship. Do not conform any longer to the pattern of this world, but be transformed by the renewing of your mind. Then you will be able to test and approve what God's will is – his good, pleasing and perfect will."*

God is going to be faithful in guiding and directing one's life in His perfect plan that He has for us. It all becomes one's personal responsibility to let God lead and direct their life.

BIGGEST CHALLENGE

As Camp Forest Springs worked on developing a continued long-range plan, it became obvious that the Camp Forest Springs site was NOT the best location to create a large year-round facility. At that time a study done by American Camping Association (ACA), showed that a facility of around 300 beds was a very efficient operating size. To get to the next level of good efficiency would be somewhere in the neighborhood of 600 beds.

With the camp being located in north central Wisconsin, the decision was made to keep the Camp Forest Springs site at the top end of the efficiency curve with somewhere between 300-400 beds. A concern growing out of that decision was that if a limit for growth was put on the organization, two things could happen:

- Limit God in what He wanted to do in the future
- Establishing a growth limit which could cause all future planning to lose momentum

To counter the two negative concerns, a decision was made to be open to expanding into other areas of the upper Midwest, by reproducing ourselves, our philosophy of camping, and taking different types of facilities closer to our constituents. We opened ourselves up to reproducing Camp Forest Springs as a year-round camp in other upper Midwest states.

We also looked into developing a retreat center for multi-national groups, where three or four directors of a given nationality would be on staff. The calendar year would be divided up into four equal time periods, with each director having a time slot for their nationality – i.e., Korean – the Korean director would have a fourth of the year to run Korean retreats, specially designed for their specific needs.

The other concept was to develop an adult retreat facility. This would require very little programming by the facility staff, but the staff would be the host people to care for those using the facility.

A committee of camp friends outside of camp board members and camp staff was formed to research different areas and needs for such facilities. One board member and myself were also part of the committee.

One of the committee members was a subdivision developer who had a real estate agent tell him about a perfect property for sale that would make a good retreat site. As we began to look into the property, it became apparent that the location, the facility, and the site would fit the requirements we had for an adult retreat facility.

We began to do a study with friends of camp, participating churches, and demographic research to determine if it really was a good fit. We made many phone calls to church leaders, asking them if they had a need for such a facility if it were to be based on the philosophy of Camp Forest Springs. Time and again we heard this response, "How soon will it be open and how do we book a retreat?"

The property included 80 acres, an unfinished lodge of about 34,000 square feet, and a model home that the developer of the 3,000 acre golf course/condominium complex had built and never finished. So we began to pursue the purchase of the property.

Prior to a board meeting where the purchase of the property would be discussed, I received a phone call from the committee member who was the developer, saying, "Yesterday my wife and I purchased the property. We have no plan for it. If Camp Forest Springs wants the property, you can have it at no cost." Well, as one would expect, it didn't take long for the board of directors to vote to accept the offer made to us!

So why is this project one of my biggest challenges?

Thinking that in just a couple years we could have the new adult conference center up and running, God had other plans for all of us. He had a real test of faith for us to see if we would really trust Him for His timing in things or if we would just go out on our own.

For the next twelve years, we struggled in getting the facility finished off. We put in all new insulation, concrete for floors in the lower level, built a maintenance shop, recreation field and a motel unit that could hold up to 99 people, plus two additional meeting rooms.

As a procedure for money management, Camp Forest Springs has desired to do development of new projects without borrowing money or having minimal loans, if we did borrow. It was our desire to hold to that principle in this new adventure.

What we were not prepared for was to learn that the friends of camp who were involved in the main site, didn't quickly catch the vision for the new site, and their financial response was very minimal. Beyond the gift of the property, we were launching out into a new million dollar plus project without the base of support that we expected.

About eight years into the project, discussion of the future of the property was placed on the agenda for the board of directors. Although one option was to sell the property, the board voted, instead, to move ahead by keeping the property, recognizing that it was God Who gave it to us.

From that day on, God began to move the project faster than we could have imagined. Today, the facility is debt-free, income is exceeding expenses, and there is a waiting list for group usage for most of the year in advance. After just three years of operation, yearly attendance is now exceeding 5000 individuals. Today, we are making plans to more than double the bed capacity.

What did I learn from this struggle of twelve years? God's time is the best time. He is never too early and never too late. When we believe He is too late for our human plans, we run ahead of Him and mess things up. Then we wonder why God isn't working.

WHAT WORDS WOULD I SHARE WITH A NEW DIRECTOR?

Most importantly is to make sure that the position you have accepted is truly a position that God wants you in. Make sure it is not something you are seeking after for yourself or as an ego trip. Then, after you are convinced that God placed you in the position, seek to let God do the directing, the guiding and the leading in all of your decisions and the decisions of the camp.

Regarding your relationship with a board of directors, realize that a manager-type personality generally does much better with an operational-type board. On the other hand, an executive/director type personality does much better with a policy-type board.

Here are some operational things that should be a priority for a new director/manager:

- Make sure you have the paperwork proving that the organization is an IRS-approved not-for-profit.
- Make sure you have all the legal documents showing ownership of the property.
- Make sure all the paperwork is up-to-date with any and all banks.
- Make sure you have a working philosophy and mission statement and that the board of directors has reviewed it and is fully supportive of it.
- Make sure you know who owns any and all items in the camp, i.e., past staff, present staff, friends of camp, and that you have an agreement to use the items and who is responsible for replacement if damage occurs.

- Make sure you have your seven day prayer list up-to-date and that you are praying over it daily.

CHAPTER 27

Leading Through Change

THE MANAGEMENT MYTH:
A widespread misunderstanding is that leading and
managing are one and the same. Up until a few years ago,
books that claimed to be on leadership were often really
about management. The main difference between the two is
that leadership is about influencing people to follow, while
management focuses on maintaining systems and processes.
As former Chrysler chairman and CEO Lee Iacocca wryly
commented, "Sometimes even the best manager is like the
little boy with the big dog, waiting to see where the dog
wants to go so that he can take him there." The best way
to test whether a person can lead rather than just manage
is to ask him to create positive change. Managers can
maintain direction, but often they can't change it. Systems
and processes can do only so much. To move people in a new
direction, you need influence.

John Maxwell - *The 21 Irrefutable Laws of Leadership*

If you have been put to sleep thinking your camp will always be a vibrant, living, growing camp, you need to wake up. Nothing lasts forever. Just the thought that your camp and its programs have a determined shelf life should make you want to keep reinventing programs and facility use.

Atrophy sets in on all things: People – Buildings– Programs – Menus – Processes– Procedures– Technology. It is all dying a slow death.

According to Peter Drucker:

> "If an organization does not change, it may stagnate and die, thus losing continuity. In order to achieve continuity, therefore, an organization must be designed to change. That continuity and change are a continuum, and not opposites, may at first seem counterintuitive to you, as it once did to me."

As a consultant, I visit many camps. I hear their stories. I see their buildings. I try to understand how their camp functions. How their boards govern. I get the big picture.

Usually, I am called in because of the lack of growth, lack of vision, lack of money, and plenty of old buildings. They are desperate for change. They usually listen and set themselves on a new course.

However, I usually don't get a call from a camp who is getting by. Getting by because of loyalty from their churches. Getting by because a few donors continue to uphold the operation of the camp. Getting by with stagnant summer programs that offer an occasional twist to satisfy the curious 11-year-old. These are the camps that are 10 years out from calling me for help. But they need help now to restore their operation to something sustainable. It is very hard to breathe life into a dying fish… and it doesn't take long for a dead fish to smell.

You have been to them; camps that smell. They smell old, damp, mildewy, and like your grandmother's house she has lived in all her life. "Ewww," is your first response. They waited too long. But you want to know the sad part? It wasn't more than 20 years ago that this camp was a great camp full of groups and young campers.

They forgot to change.

In reality, they did not want to change. Change is hard. Absolutely no one likes change. Little boys don't like to change their underwear, and big boys don't want to change their systems or methodology. And without change atrophy sets in with its gradual decay. It never happens in one year. Sometimes it doesn't become evident until it's too late; whenever guests stop coming to camp.

How can we lead through change? Look to the ant, you sluggard. He carries one piece of sand at a time and eventually over the years he builds up something great. It is the little things that keep programs and buildings fresh. It is the little additions to the playground and the housing units that tell people you are looking and aware of their needs. Does it all need a total makeover today? Probably, but you can't do it that way. Like in the movie, *What about Bob...* it is all about baby steps. Every year, tweak, adjust, rearrange, and revamp something. And after a few years, start over again and do it again. It never stops, even when you become big and bright and the best camp in the state.

Peter Drucker says it best:

> *"Developing a process of systematic abandonment, and making it a regular part of the culture of an organization,*

is one of the most effective ways to eliminate the old and make room for the new."

Joseph A. Maciariello - *A Year with Peter Drucker: 52 Weeks of Coaching for Leadership Effectiveness*

Develop a process. A process that starts with the question, "Why?" Why are we doing evening chapels this way? Why do we expect kids to carry their food and drink without a tray? Why do we allow counselors to leave on Friday without a closing debriefing session? Why do we leave the tractors parked outside the shop area? Why are we keeping five horses around that we can't use?

You have to be curious. You have to have an attitude of never being content. You have to be available to ask enough questions to finally reach a great conclusion. Asking WHY will increase your workload.

I love traditions. Traditions are an expected element of camp: the chocolate chip cookies, the cinnamon rolls, the wrangler's breakfast down by the lake, the minnow race, the carpet ball tournament, and the Saturday night kettle corn during family camps. Remove just one of these traditions and you will have a riot. Don't touch them regardless how hokey they seem to you; your guests have grown up doing this and they are expecting their children and their grandchildren to experience the same thing.

What can you change? What will repeat guests allow you to change?

We kept hearing our family campers saying, "All we do is eat–big breakfast, lunch and a big supper. I feel stuffed." We were also hearing, "Family camp is getting expensive." We adjusted our schedule by combining breakfast and lunch and serving it at 10 a.m. We still heard complaints about children getting hungry way before brunch, so we put out free cereal and milk for the early riser who needed something in their belly when they woke up. We accomplished the change rather quickly and without alienating any guests, and we lowered the cost and the workload of the kitchen staff.

We hand out retreat surveys after every one of our programmed retreats. We have a sportsmen's retreat each spring with over 600 men. Some men have not liked the speaker or the band we have used over the years. They told us, and we changed. We have two chapel services with two speakers and two bands running concurrently now. Your guests' comments should be the driving force that causes you to re-evaluate and then re-imagine your operation. When people care enough to complain and write it down, you need to not brush it off as belly-aching, but look at it as an opportunity to grow better.

The apple cart was not built in a day, so the last thing the new director wants to do is to upset the cart in his first month on the job. Know which wars you can win beforehand, and know that if you lose the war you might lose your job. Pick your fights carefully.

CHAPTER 28

Stay Put

"For I know the plans I have for you," declares the LORD, "plans to prosper you and not to harm you, plans to give you hope and a future."

Jeremiah 29:11

I know today's worker doesn't stay put for very long. According to *Forbes* magazine, the average worker stays 4.4 years on the job. I would assume for millennials the average would be even lower.

4.4 years only give you enough time to know what you don't know about running a camp. It takes at least 4.4 years to grasp the culture. It takes 4.4 years to begin to feel like you own your job. It takes 4.4 years to know where all the lift stations are located.

That is why I stayed put.

In an article written by pastor and author, Carey Nieuwhof, he discusses the first four years of those who enter into the ministry:

Year One: You're a Rock Star. *"You're smart. You see the organization through new eyes. You bring insights and*

211

practices others on the team don't have. Your star is rising and you're the hero du jour."

Year Two: Everyone's So Glad You're Here. *"Now you have a track record and people trust you. You're appreciated and appear to have staying power."*

Year Three: This Feels Like Normal. *"You've solved a lot of the problems you set out to solve. Now your bag of tricks is running a little thin. In fact, you're starting to see problems that not only other people can't solve, but you're not sure how to solve. Maybe…just maybe…you created a few of your own."*

Year Four: What's That Wall Over There? *"You don't want to say it out loud. But there's a wall ahead. And if you're honest, you know the wall is you. You are up against all your limits, your ghosts, your fears and you realize that if you're going to make progress you're going to have to grow as a person. Because you've changed everything else. Now all that's left to change is you."*

"So now, as a leader, you have a choice. You can jump out of the organization. Go find a new job — rinse, lather, repeat. Be a rock star for a year (they'll love your talents as the last guys did), let things become normal, hit a wall, and then decide to move on again."

Nieuwhof is right. Rinse, lather and become a new rock star. But let me remind you, rock stars who don't grow and change end up singing the same hit tune all their lives. Rock stars who do not re-invent themselves as they grow older end up singing Beach Boys songs on state fair stages in their late 60s, complete with wrinkles, sags, and straggly long hair. And it ain't pretty.

Besides, you really don't become a rock star after one year in a camp. After one year you should begin to feel inadequate. You should know just how much you don't know. You should begin to realize the need to seek out a mentor to help you through the next three years. You had better be attending CCCA conferences and sectional events. It is there you will rub shoulders with camp rock stars who know the ropes and can help you make sense of you and your particular situation.

Fred Remington, the famous cowboy artist from the late 1800's once wrote describing a grueling 51 mile canoe trip down the Oswegatchie River in New York, "The zest of the whole thing lies in not knowing the difficulties beforehand." That truly is the secret of staying put; having enough unknowns ahead to solve and push through to make your ministry fresh every morning, complete with new challenges and new opportunities to learn something new.

Boredom is the killer of longevity in any ministry. Boredom eats at the soul of every man. In some ways, it is the beauty of camp life. There is enough variety, enough challenges that a director should never get bored if he truly engages 100% into the ministry. If there is not a building to build, there should be a program to dissect and re-imagine. If there is not a bathroom to remodel there should be a donor to visit or a newsletter to be written or a report that tries to paint a picture of what is around the next bend in camp life. The zest IS in the unknown.

When you analyze long-term camp life, it can move into boring after a few years. Summer camp, fall retreats, getting ready for summer camp, hiring summer staff, writing curriculum for summer staff, winter retreats, summer camp, fall retreats... you get the picture. Same old, same old. After a few years, it is easy to run on auto-pilot, because you know how to do camp well enough. You can disengage yourself from digging deeper into making the camp grow and prosper by finding challenges through hobbies or outside interests.

I was feeling this after the first few years. I went for an interview to teach high school English in Alaska. I didn't get the job. At the 15-year mark, I studied and received an Iowa real estate license. At one point I approached the local realtor and asked if I might try this full-time. For some unknown reason, I stayed put. (The unknown reason really came down to the fact that enough people were praying for me). I fell back into a rhythm of camp, committed to push through the wall of repetition and boredom. The last 16 years have proved to be the most fruitful and rewarding years of my camp career.

Within this book you have read other directors' stories. Each of them endured the lean years, each of them met new challenges and solved the next big problem. And each of them stayed long enough to produce a legacy that will outlive their time here on earth; they have built up a movement and created an institution that runs without them.

Stay focused. Keep leading so others will follow. Keep paddling. Never give up... for truly, there is zest around the next bend of the river!

APPENDIX

WHAT'S ON MY KINDLE?

A Leader Thinks Aloud by Dr. Glenn Brooke

A Sense of Urgency by John Kotter

A Year with Peter Drucker by Joseph Maciariello

Be a People Person by John Maxwell

Be All You Can Be by John Maxwell

Benjamin Franklin by Walter Isaacson

Beyond Boundaries by Dr. John Townsend

Billy Graham by David Frost

Bold by Peter Diamandis and Steven Kotler

Boundaries by Dr. Henry Cloud and Dr. John Townsend

Boundaries for Leaders by Dr. Henry Cloud

Cyropaedia: the Education of Cyrus by Xenophon

Everybody Matters by Bob Chapman

Daring Greatly by Brene Brown

Deep Influence by T.J. Addington

Do Over by Jon Acuff

Drive by Daniel Pink

Enough by John Bogle

Exceptional Service Exceptional Profit by Leonardo Inghelleri

Execution by Larry Bossidy and Ram Charan

Essentialism by Greg Mckeown

Falling Forward by John Maxwell

5 Levels of Leadership by John Maxwell

Good Leaders ask Great Questions by John Maxwell

Great by Choice by Jim Collins

Grit by Paul Stoltz

Hiring Smart by Dr. Pierre Mornell

Home Run by Kevin Myers

How Successful People Lead by John Maxwell

How High will you Climb by John Maxwell

Integrity by Dr. Henry Cloud

John Adams by David McCullough

Leaders Eat Last by Simon Sinek

Leadership Briefs by Dick Daniels

Leadership Beyond Reason by Dr. John Townsend

Leading Change without Losing It by Carey Nieuwhof

1776 by David McCullough

Managing Transitions by William Bridges

Mastering the Management Buckets by John Pearson

Man's Search for Meaning by Viktor Frankl

Morning on Horseback by David McCullough

Multipliers by Liz Wiseman

Necessary Endings by Dr. Henry Cloud

Nine Minutes on Monday by James Robbins

9 Things a Leader Must Do by Dr. Henry Cloud

Reinventing Organizations by Frederic Laloux

Seabiscuit by Laura Hillenbrand

Servant Leadership by Robert Greenleaf

Setting the Table by Danny Meyer

Simple Sabotage by Robert Galford

Start with Why by Simon Sinek

Strengths Based Leadership by Tom Rath and Barry Conchie

Switch- How to Change Things when Change is Hard by Chip and Dan Heath

The Coaching Habit by Michael Stanier

The Effective Executive by Peter Drucker

The Emperor's Handbook by Marcus Aurelius

The 15 Invaluable Laws of Growth by John Maxwell

The New Gold Standard by Joseph Michelli

The Noticer by Andy Andrews

The 21 Irrefutable Laws of Leadership by John Maxwell

The Speed of Trust by Stephen Covey

The System of the World by Isaac Newton

The 360 Leader by John Maxwell

Today Matters by John Maxwell

The Wright Brothers by David McCullough

The Attacker's Advantage by Ram Charan

The New One Minute Manager by Ken Blanchard

The Nordstrom Way by Robert Spector

The Power of Full Engagement by Jim Loehr and Tony Schwartz

The 7 Habits of Highly Effective People by Stephen R. Covey

Truman by David McCullough

Turn the Ship Around by L. David Marquet

Unbroken by Laura Hillenbrand

Wooden by John Wooden

Work the System by Sam Carpenter

The author can be reached at
earldtaylor@yahoo.com.
"I am available for consulting, coaching, or for workshops and seminars."

The author is also organizing an interim-directors program to fill the gap as camps transition from one leader to another.

You can follow the author on his blog:
www.beallyoucouldbe.wordpress.com